SCIENCE SCOPE
BIOLOGY

Mark Winterbottom
Ceri Jones

Hodder & Stoughton

A MEMBER OF THE HODDER HEADLINE GROUP

Contents

Preface

Biology is a fascinating subject. It has a direct influence on all our lives, and is at the forefront of modern technology. Without biology, there would be fewer medicines, less food in the supermarkets, and many more animals and plants would have become extinct. We have written this book in the hope that pupils will recognise and understand some of the basic principles of biology. Such an understanding should also help pupils develop reasoned viewpoints on controversial issues in biology which affect us all.

This book provides extensive cover for pupils in Years 7, 8 and 9 following the Life and Living Processes section of the Key Stage 3 Science National Curriculum or the Common Entrance Examination at 13+ Science Syllabus (Life Processes and Living Things).

Particular attention has been paid to the inclusion of extension material, which will aid pupils of average and above average abilities, who are aiming for a high level of achievement.

The following features have been included in the book:

- Test Yourself Questions to consolidate and reinforce understanding.
- Extension Boxes, which contain material aimed specifically at those pupils aiming for the higher tiers or following the Common Entrance examination.
- Summaries bring together all the ideas in the chapter.
- End-of-Chapter Questions provide opportunities to apply knowledge from the topic. Questions that refer to material covered in the extension boxes are on a yellow tinted background.

We hope you have as much fun reading this book as we have had in writing it.

Acknowledgements

Our thanks to all at Hodder and Stoughton for their help in producing this book and in particular to Charlotte Litt for seeing the book through all its stages. Our wives also deserve a big thank you, for their enthusiasm and support throughout the project.

Mark Winterbottom and Ceri Jones

Matching Grid

	National Curriculum Programme of Study	Key Stage 3 Scheme of Work	Common Entrance Examination 13 +
Chapter 1 Cells	1a, 1b, 1e	7A	1a, 1b, 1e
Chapter 2 Specialised cells	1a, 1c, 1d, 1e, 2g	7A	1a, 1c, 1d, 1e, 2g
Chapter 3 Food and digestion	2a, 2b, 2c, 2d	8A	2a, 2b, 2c, 2d
Chapter 4 Fit and healthy	2e	9B	2e
Chapter 5 Reproduction	2f, 2g, 2h	7B	2f, 2g, 2h
Chapter 6 Breathing and respiration	2i	8B	2i
Chapter 7 Health and drugs	2i, 2m, 2n	9B	2i, 2m, 2n
Chapter 8 Microbes and disease	2n	8C	2n
Chapter 9 Photosynthesis	3a, 3b, 3e	9C, 9D	3a, 3b, 3e
Chapter 10 Adaptations for photosynthesis	3c, 3d	9C, 9D	3c, 3d
Chapter 11 Variation and Inheritance	4a, 4c	7D, 9A	4a, 4c
Chapter 12 Classification	4b	7C, 7D, 8D	4b
Chapter 13 Feeding relationships	5e, 5f	8D	5e, 5f
Chapter 14 Habitats	5a, 5b, 5c, 5d	8D, 9D	5a, 5b, 5c, 5d

1 Cells and living things

Imagine you are an alien and have just arrived from Mars. How would you know which things were alive and which were not? Living things can be very varied.

Some living things do not really look as if they are alive at all.

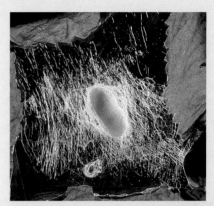

So what makes something living? Some of these look like, or appear to behave like, living things, but are they really living?

This chapter examines what it means to be alive. It looks at what living things are made of, and it introduces you to the microscope, an essential tool in the study of living things.

What does it mean to be alive?

Living things (**organisms**) all share the same seven characteristics. If something does not have even one of these characteristics, it is not a living organism. You can remember these characteristics by looking at their first letters. They spell the word MRS GREN.

Movement	Going from one place to another
Respiration	Releasing energy from food
Sensitivity	Reacting to the environment
Growth	Getting bigger
Reproduction	Making new living things
Excretion	Getting rid of waste
Nutrition	Getting food

Test Yourself

1 Things that are not living do not have all of the seven features. For each of the following, explain which feature (or features) is missing: a) teddy bear, b) car, c) bouncing ball.

2 Explain why the stick insect in the picture is a living thing.

What are living organisms made of?

Living organisms are made of **organs**. Organs are parts of the body that help a living thing to carry out all the processes needed to stay alive. Look at Figure 1 showing some of the organs in the human body. Each one has a different job.

Organs often work closely together in an **organ system**. For example, there are several organs in the digestive system which work together to process food. There are several other organ systems in the human body including the breathing system, the circulatory system, the nervous system and the excretory system which gets rid of waste products.

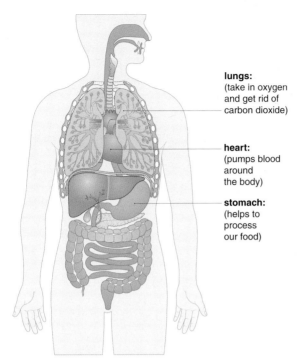

lungs:
(take in oxygen
and get rid of
carbon dioxide)

heart:
(pumps blood
around
the body)

stomach:
(helps to
process
our food)

Figure 1 ▲   Three of the most important organs in the human body

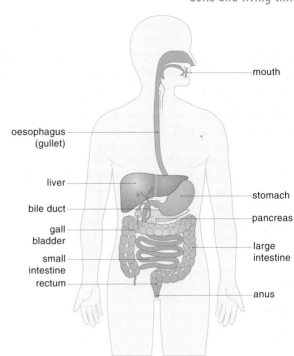

mouth

oesophagus
(gullet)

liver

bile duct

gall
bladder

small
intestine
rectum

stomach

pancreas

large
intestine

anus

Figure 2 ▲   All these organs work together in the digestive system

Figure 3 ▼   Some of the major organ systems in the human body

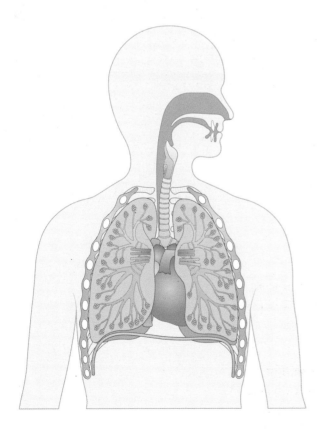

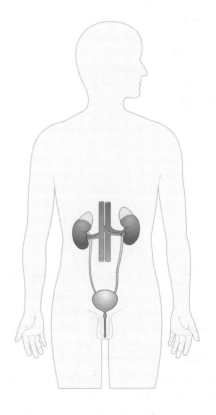

a) the breathing system

b) the excretory system

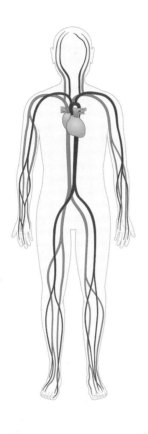

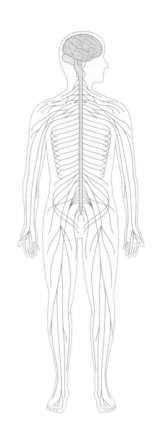

c) the circulatory system

d) the nervous system

Plants also have organs. Because plants are not as active as animals, it is easy to forget that they are also living things. Look at Figure 4 to see how a plant's organs help it to stay alive.

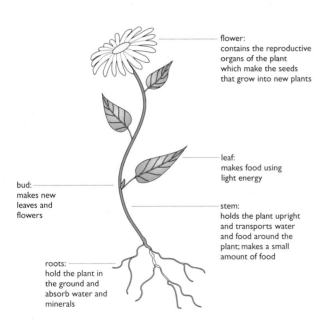

flower:
contains the reproductive
organs of the plant
which make the seeds
that grow into new plants

leaf:
makes food using
light energy

bud:
makes new
leaves and
flowers

stem:
holds the plant upright
and transports water
and food around the
plant; makes a small
amount of food

roots:
hold the plant in
the ground and
absorb water and
minerals

Figure 4 ◄ Some of the organs in a plant

Extension box

Organ transplants

The person in the picture has a kidney that does not work properly. The kidney's job is to clean her blood. If her blood is not clean, she will die. There are two ways in which doctors can help her to stay alive.

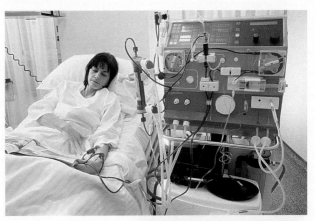

1 They can divert her blood through a dialysis machine which acts like an artificial kidney. The blood leaves her body through a tube, passes through the machine and returns to her body. Whilst inside the machine, the blood is cleaned. This can be costly, and is very time-consuming for the patient.

2 They can put a new healthy kidney into her body. About 1500 kidney transplants are carried out in Britain each year. The healthy kidneys come from people who have died. Many people carry a donor card which says that doctors can use their organs for transplant if they die.

Gardeners also use organ transplants on plants. They can remove the bud from one plant and attach it to another. To help it to become part of the new plant, they cut a small hole in the plant and push it in. They then wrap tape around the two until they grow together.

Organs themselves are made of **cells**. Cells are the building blocks of all living things. Your whole body is made of cells. Cells are so small, you can only see them using a microscope.

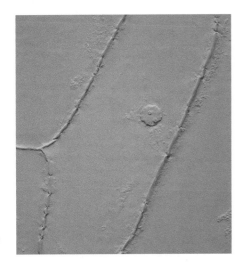

a)

b)

Figure 5 ▲   Plant and animal cells look very different when seen under a light microscope (a) onion epidermis cells b) human cheek cells

3   Which of life's characteristics are the following organ systems involved in: a) digestive system, b) locomotory system, c) excretory system.

4   Which two organs in plants are most directly involved in nutrition?

5   Which organ controls the human body?

6   What are the building blocks of all living things?

Figure 6 ▲   A light microscope

How does a microscope work?

There are several different types of **microscopes**. They all look slightly different, but they all have similar parts that do the same job. Figure 6 shows you what those parts are called.

You see an object when light from that object enters your eye. Microscopes make things appear larger by changing the light before it enters your eye. They do this by using lenses. The lenses **magnify** what you are looking at (the **specimen**).

It is important that you know how much larger the specimen appears than it actually is (the total **magnification**). This will depend on the magnification of the objective lens and the eyepiece lens. To calculate the total magnification, use this formula:

$$\text{total magnification} = \text{eyepiece lens magnification} \times \text{objective lens magnification}$$

You will find the magnification of each lens written on the side or the top of the lens.

To really understand how a microscope works, you need to follow the pathway of light. Light bounces off the mirror so it travels straight upwards, through the hole in the stage and through the specimen. If the specimen were too thick, light would not get through it, so it is important to have a thin specimen. Having passed through the specimen, light travels through the objective lens and the eyepiece lens into your eye.

When you look down the microscope, you see a disc of light called the **field of view**. Within that field of view, you will see your specimen. To help see specimens more clearly, it is often a good idea to add some coloured dye called a stain.

Ideas and Evidence

The invention of the microscope

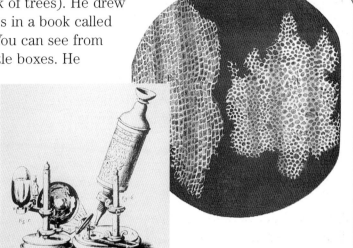

In 1665, Robert Hooke invented the first microscope. He used it to examine cork (which comes from the bark of trees). He drew what he could see and published the pictures in a book called *Micrographia* (this means small pictures). You can see from Hooke's drawings that he saw lots of tiny little boxes. He called them 'cells' because they reminded him of the rooms that monks lived in (*cell* means *little room* in Latin).

Since then, people have discovered new and more effective stains and have invented machines for slicing thin specimens accurately. Combined with better lenses, these improvements have allowed scientists to magnify objects by over 1000 times.

Extension box

The electron microscope

To look at very small things, scientists use an electron microscope. This is a very expensive type of microscope, which uses tiny particles called electrons instead of light to see the specimen. After the electrons pass through the specimen, they hit a special screen. Wherever an electron hits the screen, the screen gives off a tiny amount of light. This produces a picture of the specimen on the screen.

An electron microscope can magnify a specimen by up to 500 000 times. If we made you look 500 000 times larger, you would appear to be about 400 miles high!

Test Yourself

7   What is magnification?

8   How do you work out the total magnification produced by the objective and the eyepiece lenses?

9   Where on the microscope do you put your specimen?

How to use the microscope

To look at a specimen under the microscope you need to follow the instructions below.

1 Cut a very thin slice of your specimen, or peel a very thin layer from your specimen.
2 Lay it on a microscope slide (a thin piece of glass).
3 Add one drop of water or stain. The stain makes the specimen easier to see.
4 Lower a cover slip slowly over the specimen as shown in the diagram. This stops air bubbles forming.

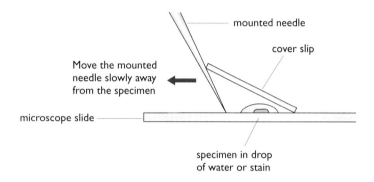

Figure 7 ▲ Preparing a microscope slide

5 Place the slide on the microscope stage with the specimen in the centre of the stage.
6 Twist the objective lenses so the shortest lens is pointing downwards.
7 Twist the focus knob so the distance between the slide and objective lens is the smallest it can be.
8 Look through the eyepiece lens and twist the focus knob towards you until the specimen comes into focus.
9 If you want to magnify the specimen even more, twist the objective lenses until a larger lens is pointing downwards. Look through the eyepiece lens and twist the fine focus knob until the specimen comes into focus.

Having prepared your specimen, you may want to show someone else what it looks like. If they are standing next to you, they can just have a look down the microscope. If they live in a different place, however, you will need to record what you see. The best way to do this is to take a picture using a camera attached to the microscope, but microscope cameras are very expensive. Because of this, you will usually have to draw your specimen. This is more difficult than it looks. Look at Figure 8. This is a very bad drawing of what someone has seen under the microscope. The teacher has indicated what is wrong with it alongside.

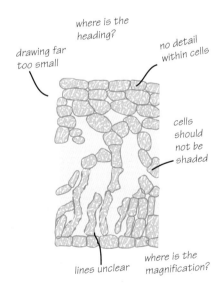

Figure 8 ▲ How **not** to draw what you see under the microscope

Extension box

Examining cheek cells under the microscope

You can use a microscope to look at some of your own cheek cells. To do this you should follow the instructions below:

1　Use a cotton bud to wipe around the inside of your cheek.
2　Dab the cotton bud onto a microscope slide.
3　Put the cotton bud into disinfectant.
4　Add one drop of methylene blue stain to make the nucleus and other parts of the cell show up.
5　Continue preparing the specimen as usual (from point number 4 in the list of instructions on page 8).

Extension box

Estimating the size of your specimen

When you look at a specimen using a microscope, it appears larger than it actually is. So how do you work out its actual size. You can get a good idea by using a ruler. Before you prepare your specimen, look at a ruler under the microscope. Measure the width of the field of view in millimetres. When you look at your specimen, you can estimate how far across the field of view it stretches. You can use this to work out how big your specimen is. For example, in the picture, the field of view is 1.5 mm wide. The specimen stretches across half of the field of view. Therefore:

Length of the specimen = ½ × 1.5 mm = 0.75 mm

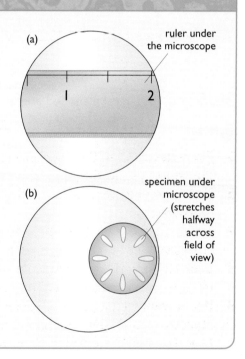

(a) ruler under the microscope

(b) specimen under microscope (stretches halfway across field of view)

Test Yourself

10　When you first look at a specimen under the microscope, which objective lens should you use?

11　Why might you use a stain when preparing your specimen?

12　Make a list of six rules you should follow when drawing a specimen under the microscope.

What do cells look like?

Look at the plant and animal cells in Figure 9. Plant cells and animal cells are slightly different. Both plant and animal cells have a nucleus, a cell membrane and cytoplasm. However, only plant cells have chloroplasts, a cell wall and a vacuole.

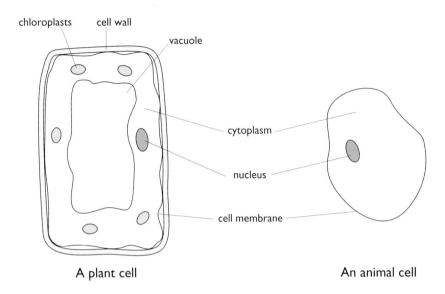

A plant cell   An animal cell

Figure 9 ▲   A typical plant and animal cell

The drawings in Figure 9 make cells look like they are flat. In reality they are not flat. Plant cells are a bit like boxes and animal cells are a bit like bags. When you look at a cell under a microscope, it is like cutting the cell in half and looking at the cut end (see Figure 10).

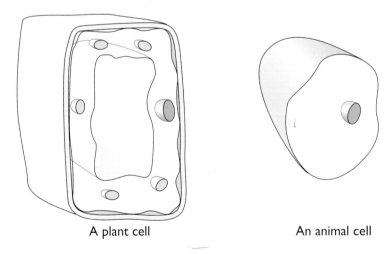

A plant cell   An animal cell

Figure 10 ▲

All the parts of the cells have different jobs, which help to keep the cells alive. Look at the spider diagram to find out what they do.

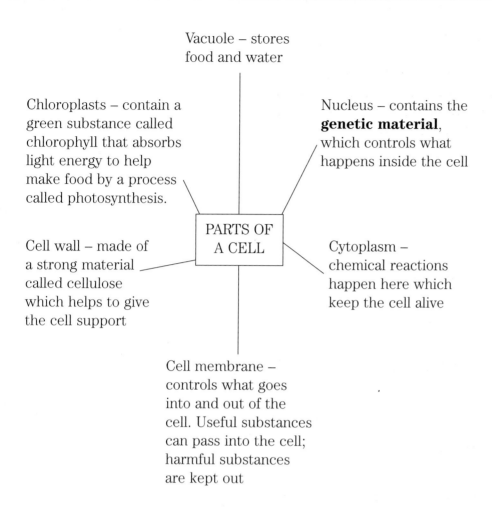

Vacuole – stores food and water

Chloroplasts – contain a green substance called chlorophyll that absorbs light energy to help make food by a process called photosynthesis.

Nucleus – contains the **genetic material**, which controls what happens inside the cell

PARTS OF A CELL

Cell wall – made of a strong material called cellulose which helps to give the cell support

Cytoplasm – chemical reactions happen here which keep the cell alive

Cell membrane – controls what goes into and out of the cell. Useful substances can pass into the cell; harmful substances are kept out

Extension box

Genes and DNA

The instructions inside the nucleus are contained in a chemical called deoxyribonucleic acid (**DNA**). DNA forms long chains, which coil up a little like telephone wires. There are 46 chains of DNA within the nucleus of each human cell. These are made up of 23 pairs. Along each chain are the instructions that run the cell. Each instruction is called a **gene**. To actually control what happens in each cell, the instructions in the gene must be translated into proteins.

Genes not only affect the appearance and behaviour of each cell, they also affect the whole organism. For example, you have a gene controlling your eye colour. If you have brown eyes, you have a gene in all of your cells which makes a particular protein. This protein makes the brown pigment in your eyes.

Ideas and Evidence   The cell theory

After Robert Hooke produced his book *Micrographia*, more and more scientists started to use microscopes. Gradually microscopy (the use of microscopes) became more sophisticated. By 1838, many plants and animals had been examined under the microscope.

Matthias Jakob Schleiden (in 1838) and Theodor Schwann (in 1839) realised that all plants and animals were made of cells, and that individual cells were alive and could reproduce. You will learn how they reproduce in the next chapter. This **cell theory** changed the way that scientists thought about living things for ever.

Extension box

Cells without a nucleus

Bacteria are living things that cause disease and make things go mouldy. Another name for bacteria is *prokaryotes* (this means *before nucleus*). They are each made of only one cell, and these cells look a little like plant cells. However, there are some very obvious differences which you can see in the diagram. Instead of having a nucleus, the instructions for running a prokaryote cell are found in the cytoplasm.

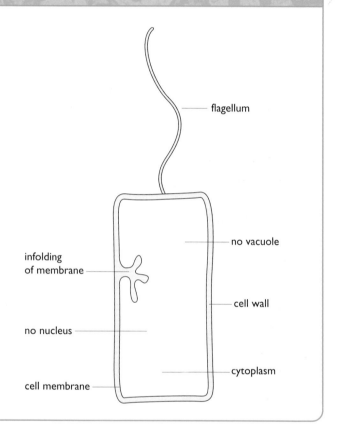

Test Yourself

13 What is the job of a) the cell membrane and b) the vacuole?

14 List three differences between plant cells and animal cells.

15 Plants do not eat food. Which part of the cell helps them to make food?

Summary

When you have finished studying this chapter, you should understand that:

✓ Living organisms all share seven characteristics: movement, reproduction, sensitivity, growth, respiration, excretion and nutrition.

✓ All living things are made of organs, which do different jobs to keep the organism alive.

✓ Organs work together with other organs in organ systems.

✓ Living things are made of cells and cells are the basic units of life.

✓ Microscopes are used to look at things that are too small to see with the naked eye, such as cells.

✓ There are differences and similarities between animal and plant cells.

✓ The different parts of animal and plant cells have specific functions.

End-of-Chapter Questions

1   Explain in your own words the following key terms you have met in this chapter:

organism

organ

organ system

cell

genetic material

microscope

magnify

specimen

magnification

field of view

DNA

gene

cell theory

2   Explain why the following things are not living:

a) candle flame

b) airplane

c) loudspeaker

3   Name one organ in a) the reproductive system, b) the nervous system and c) the excretory system.

4   You are looking at something using an objective lens (×40 magnification) and an eyepiece lens (×10 magnification). What is the total magnification?

5   Draw a flow chart to describe the pathway of light through a microscope.

6   Write an instruction manual for the microscope you have been using. Think about what the reader will need to know to be able to use the microscope effectively.

7   Imagine you have been shrunk down so you can walk inside a plant cell. Describe your journey into the cell, through the cell and out the other side. You should describe what you see and explain the function of each part.

Your house is probably made of bricks. Bricks are used to build houses because they are strong and sturdy and you can stick them together with cement. If bricks are so good, why don't we use them to build the whole house? Imagine a house with brick wires, a brick bath and brick beds.

Making everything in your house out of brick will not keep it working properly. For example, brick wires will not conduct electricity, a brick bath will not hold water, and a brick bed would be very hard to sleep on. Because of this, we use different materials to build different parts of our houses.

Living things are the same. Different types of cell do different jobs. This chapter shows you how cells can be different, why they work together to do particular jobs, and how they are involved in making new living things.

Different cells, different jobs

You may think that all animal cells are identical and that all plant cells are identical. Many of the cells in Figure 1 do not look anything like the cells you met in Chapter 1. But they are all examples of animal cells or plant cells.

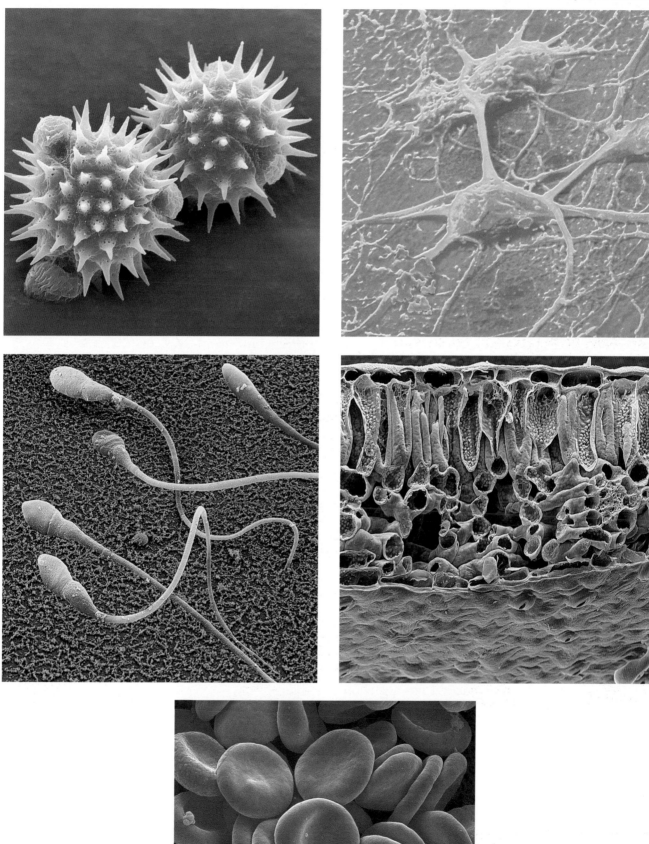

Figure 1

These cells look different from one another because they do different jobs. The shape and structure of each cell helps it to do its job properly. We say that each cell is **adapted** or specialised to doing its particular job.

Test Yourself

1   Write down whether the cell in each photo in Figure 1 is an animal cell or a plant cell.

2   Cells are adapted to doing their particular jobs. What does *adapted* mean?

Specialised cells in animals

Ciliated epithelial cell

Epithelial cells cover the surface of animals' organs. Ciliated epithelial cells are found in your trachea (windpipe) which leads to your lungs. The cilia are extensions of the cell membrane but look like tiny hairs. When you breathe in, dust from the air gets stuck in the sticky mucus in the trachea, leading down to your lungs. The cilia beat backwards and forwards, pushing the dust away from the lungs. If they did not do this, your lungs would get clogged up.

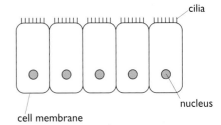

Figure 2 ▲   A ciliated epithelium cell

Egg cell (ovum)

This is the sex cell of a female animal. It carries the genetic material from the mother and joins up with the sperm cell from the father. The egg cell is very large because it contains large amounts of stored food. This food helps the cell to develop after it has fused with the sperm cell.

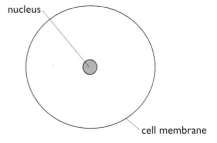

Figure 3 ▲   A human egg cell

Sperm cell

This is the sex cell of a male animal. It carries the genetic material to the egg cell of the mother. Its tail and streamlined shape help it to swim inside the female's body on its way to the egg cell. At the front of its head, it has a section called an acrosome. This contains chemical tools called enzymes, which the sperm cell uses to 'cut' its way into the egg cell.

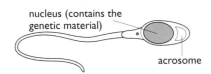

Figure 4 ▲   A human sperm cell

Red blood cell

Red blood cells carry oxygen around the body. All of the cells in our body need oxygen to make energy. Red blood cells contain a chemical called haemoglobin which carries the oxygen. To make sure the cells carry as much oxygen as possible, they have no nucleus, making room for more haemoglobin. The shape of red blood cells also helps make them efficient at their job. Their biconcave shape gives them a large **surface area**, which means oxygen can enter the cell more quickly.

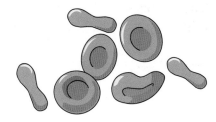

Figure 5 ▲ Red blood cells

Test Yourself

3 How is a red blood cell adapted to carrying oxygen?

4 Why are ciliated epithelial cells good at their job?

5 Write down three ways in which a sperm cell is adapted to its role in reproduction.

Specialised cells in plants

Root hair cell

Root hair cells grow out from the root just behind the root tip. These extensions give the cell a larger surface area. This means that more of its surface is in contact with the water in the soil, so the root can absorb more water from the soil.

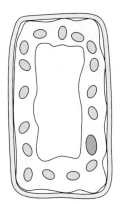

Figure 6 ▲ A root hair cell

Palisade cell

Palisade cells are found in the leaves and stems of plants. They 'catch' light from the Sun and use it to make food by photosynthesis. To help them do this, palisade cells contain lots of chloroplasts. Chloroplasts contain chlorophyll, a chemical which is good at 'catching' light energy.

Test Yourself

6 Why are root hair cells good at absorbing water?

7 Copy the picture of the palisade cell. Label it using these words: chloroplasts, nucleus, vacuole, cell wall, cell membrane, cytoplasm.

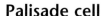

Figure 7 ▲ A palisade cell

Tissues

A group of cells that look the same and do the same job is called a **tissue**. In animals and plants, cells often work together in tissues.

Muscle tissue

Muscle cells are long and thin and are very good at pulling. One muscle cell alone could not pull very much, but lots of muscle cells working together can lift heavy weights.

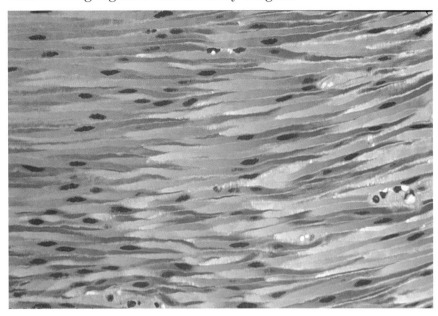

Figure 8 ◄ Muscle tissue

Epithelial tissue

In animals, epithelial cells cover and protect organs. One epithelial cell alone would not protect much, but a sheet of epithelial cells covers the whole surface of an organ.

Figure 9 ◄ Epithelial tissue

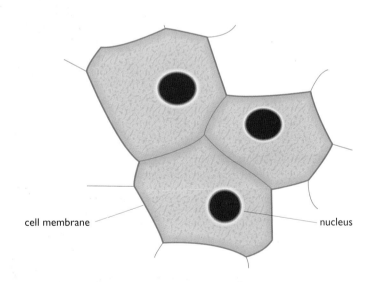

cell membrane   nucleus

Xylem tissue

Xylem cells line up end to end to form a tube which carries water around the plant. One xylem cell alone would not carry water very far, but a column of xylem cells together can carry water throughout the plant.

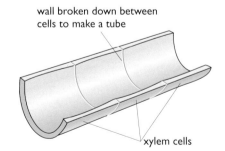

wall broken down between cells to make a tube

xylem cells

Figure 10 ▲ Xylem tissue

Test Yourself

7   What is a tissue?

8   Explain why cells work better in groups.

9   What is the job of epithelial tissue?

10 What is the job of xylem tissue?

What are organs made of?

Ideas and Evidence

Marie Bichat lived between 1771 and 1802. He was the first person to examine organs in detail, and noticed they were made up of layers. He named the layers tissues. No-one realised that tissues were made of cells until Schleiden and Schwann came up with their *cell theory* (see Chapter 1).

In the same way as cells group together to form tissues, tissues group together to form **organs**. Each tissue has a particular job to do which contributes to the overall function of the organ.

Look at the heart in Figure 11. Its job is to squeeze blood around the body. The heart is mostly made up of muscle tissue. It also has nervous tissue, which carries instructions from the brain to the muscle tissue. The instructions may tell the muscle to squeeze more quickly or more slowly.

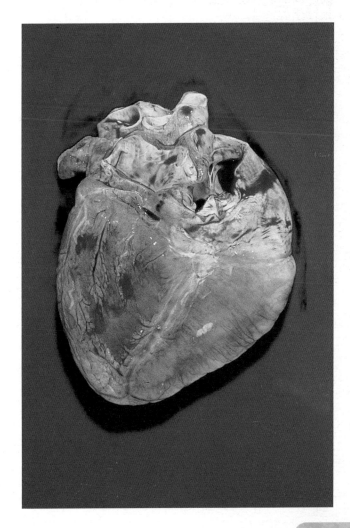

Figure 11 ▶   The human heart. You can see the blood vessels on the surface which supply the muscle tissue with food and oxygen

A root is an organ in a plant whose job is to absorb water and minerals. It has epidermal tissue through which absorption happens. Root hair cells are part of the epidermal tissue. It also has xylem tissue to carry water to the rest of the plant.

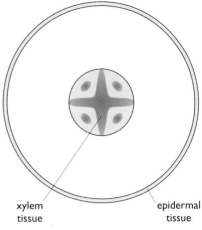

xylem
tissue

epidermal
tissue

Figure 12 ▲   A section through a plant root

Test Yourself

11 What is the job of the following organs: a) heart, b) leg and c) root?

12 Explain how the tissues in a) the heart and b) the root help the organ to do its job.

How are new living things made?

New animals are made when sex cells (**gametes**) from a male and female animal join together. You already know about sperm cells, which are the male gametes, and egg cells, which are the female gametes.

When the sperm cell enters the egg cell, the sperm nucleus joins together with the egg nucleus. This process is called **fertilisation**. Fertilisation produces the first cell of a new animal. This cell will then grow into an embryo and then into a baby.

In plants, the male gamete is not a sperm cell, but a pollen cell. Pollen cells are produced in the anthers of a plant and packaged inside pollen grains. The female gametes are the egg cells, which are found in the ovules inside the ovary of a flower. Look at Figure 13 to check you know where these structures are. For fertilisation to happen, the pollen cell must join together with the egg cell. Pollen grains are transferred from the anther of one flower to the stigma of another flower either by the wind or by insects. This process is called **pollination**.

Figure 13 ◄   The reproductive parts of a flower

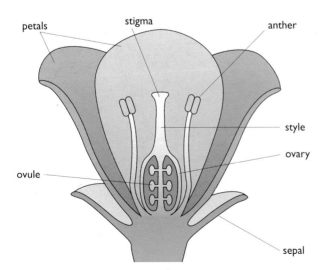

petals

stigma

anther

style

ovary

ovule

sepal

When the pollen grain lands on the stigma, it begins to produce a pollen tube, which grows into the stigma and down the style. This tube is an extension of the pollen cell. To control its growth, the pollen cell has an extra nucleus. Once it has reached the ovule, the main nucleus of the pollen cell passes down the pollen tube and joins together with the nucleus of the egg cell inside the ovule. This is fertilisation and produces the first cell of a new plant. This cell will then grow into an embryo, a seed and eventually a new plant.

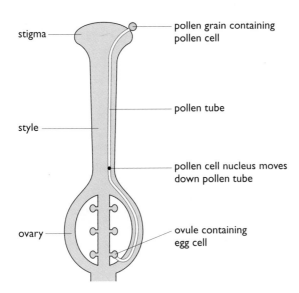

stigma —
pollen grain containing pollen cell

pollen tube

style —

pollen cell nucleus moves down pollen tube

ovary —
ovule containing egg cell

Figure 14 ◄ Fertilisation in a flowering plant

Extension box

Types of pollination

Some flowers can pollinate themselves – they **self-pollinate**. This means that pollen can drop from the anthers onto the stigma of the same flower. It then grows a pollen tube and fertilisation happens.

Most flowers do not self-pollinate – they **cross-pollinate** instead. This is because, on each flower, the anthers do not produce pollen at the same time as the stigma is ready to receive it. The pollen must therefore be transferred to the stigma of another flower. This is done by insects or by the wind. Look at the differences between wind-pollinated and insect-pollinated flowers. It is not only the flowers that look different. The pollen from insect-pollinated flowers often has little spikes on its surface to help it hold onto the insect (see Figure 1).

Test Yourself

13 What are the male gametes in a) animals and b) plants?

14 What are the female gametes in a) animals and b) plants?

15 What is fertilisation?

16 What is pollination?

17 Draw a flow chart showing how a pollen grain travels from the anther of one flower to the ovary of another.

How are new cells made?

Once fertilisation has happened, the new cell produced begins to divide. **Cell division** produces two new daughter cells, which themselves get larger and then divide again. This happens over and over again, until a whole adult organism has been produced.

Cell division is also involved in growth. Look at the picture of cells in the root in Figure 15. Some of them are much smaller than the others. The small ones have just been made by cell division. This happens when the larger cells divide into two. The two small cells will eventually get larger and then divide themselves. As the number of cells increases, the root grows.

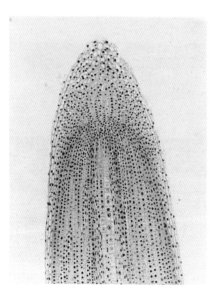

Figure 15 ◄ Dividing cells in an onion root tip

There is a little more to cell division than meets the eye. If you divided everything in the cell in half, each daughter cell would have only half a nucleus. That means it would have only half the instructions needed to run the cell. Imagine if a muscle cell divided to make two new muscle cells. If they only had half the instructions, they would not do their job properly. Because of this, the instructions in the nucleus must copy themselves before cell division. Each daughter cell gets a copy of these instructions.

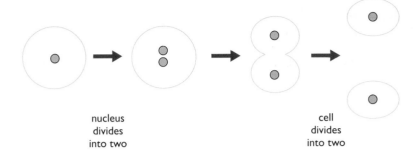

nucleus
divides
into two

cell
divides
into two

Figure 16 ▲ Cell division

Extension box

How does cell division work?

Inside the nucleus of each of your cells there are 46 chains of DNA. These chains are called chromosomes. At the beginning of cell division, these chains copy themselves. The nucleus disappears and tiny fibres form. The fibres pull one copy of each chain to different ends of the cell. The nucleus reforms around them and the cell itself then divides.

You may be wondering how gametes are made. If they had a full set of instructions in their nucleus, the cell produced after fertilisation would have two sets of instructions. Such a cell would not be able to survive. Gametes actually have only half a set of instructions. The instructions are split in half when the gametes are made during cell division. This type of cell division only happens when gametes are made.

Summary

When you have finished studying this chapter, you should understand that:

✔ Plant and animal cells can be adapted to doing particular jobs.

✔ A group of cells that look the same, and do the same job, is called a tissue.

✔ Organs are made of tissues working together.

✔ Fertilisation happens when the nuclei of sex cells join together.

✔ For fertilisation to happen in plants, the pollen must be transferred from the anther of one flower to the stigma of another in a process known as pollination.

✔ New cells are made by cell division.

End-of-Chapter Questions

1 Explain in your own words the following key terms you have met in this chapter:

adapted

surface area

tissue

organ

gamete

fertilisation

pollination

self-pollination

cross-pollination

cell division

2 For each of the following cells, write down its job, and write down one adaptation that helps it to do its job.

a) ciliated epithelial cell

b) root hair cell

c) egg cell

d) sperm cell

e) palisade cell

3 Name one tissue in a) the heart, b) the leaf and c) the leg.

4 Design an artificial cell according to the following specifications. You can include adaptations from several different cells in your design.

The cell must be able to move, have a large surface area, carry genetic information and make its own food.

5 Smoking damages the cilia on ciliated epithelium. What effect will this have on the lungs?

6 John suffers from hay fever. This is caused by pollen being blown through the air by the wind. Explain where the pollen has come from and where it is going to.

7 Guita has an apple for lunch. She sees some seeds inside. In what part of the flower did they develop?

8 Write a job description advertising the post of 'pollen cell'. The description must include all the adaptations that the pollen cell must have.

9 Using your school library, textbooks or the Internet, find out about tissue grafting. Explain what it is and when it is used.

3 Food and digestion

The sumo wrestler in the picture weighed 300 kg. He was the largest sumo wrestler in the history of the sport. In order to get this big he had to eat a huge amount of food every day.

Certainly food helps you grow bigger, but it's also involved in providing energy for your body's functions and all the complex chemical reactions that happen inside your cells. In this chapter we will find out more about how the body uses the food we eat.

A balanced diet

You eat a variety of different foods, from fruit and vegetables to meat or fish. You may be surprised to learn that they are all made of just seven different food types: proteins, carbohydrates, fats, vitamins, minerals, fibre and water. To remain healthy, we need to eat a diet which contains all seven of these food types. We call this a **balanced diet**.

Proteins

Figure 1 ◄ All these foods contain protein

In Figure 1 you can see the kinds of foods that contain a lot of **protein**. This type of food is needed for growth (making new cells) and repairing bits of your body that you might have broken. In fact, your body's cells are mainly made of protein and even your hair and fingernails are made from it!

Carbohydrates

Figure 2 ◄ All these foods contain carbohydrates

Figure 2 shows some of the foods that contain a lot of **carbohydrates**. Your body uses carbohydrates, such as glucose and starch, to release energy. The energy that's released is used for all your body's functions, such as moving, keeping warm, thinking, talking and manufacturing new cells. Without an energy supply, your body couldn't do any of these things. Eating carbohydrates is the equivalent of filling up your car with petrol. Carbohydrates are your body's favourite 'fuel'.

Fats

Figure 3 ◄ All these foods contain fats

Fats are used by your body to store energy. Fats actually contain almost twice the amount of energy per gram as carbohydrates. Your body stores fat as a layer underneath your skin which acts as an insulator and helps keep you warm on cold winter days. Fats are also important in your diet because your cell membranes are made from them; in fact, your cell membranes feel very much like olive oil to the touch!

Extension box

Although we need a certain amount of fat in our diet, eating too much fat, particularly animal fat, can be very bad for us. Doctors say that no more than 35% of our diet should be made up of fat. When large quantities of fat are consumed, the body uses what it needs and then stores the rest under the skin and around the body organs. Over time, people who continually eat more fat than they need become obese. **Obesity** is defined as excessive accumulation of body fat and causes serious health risks. Obese people are much more likely to suffer from heart attacks, strokes and cancer.

Vitamins

Vitamins are substances that are needed by your body in very small amounts to keep you healthy. They play an important part in chemical reactions inside your body but you cannot get energy from them.

There are around 16 or more different vitamins currently recognised by scientists. Most of them are known by different letters e.g. vitamin A or vitamin C. You find vitamins in lots of different foods, but fruits and vegetables are the best source for your body. Some diseases can be caused by a lack of certain vitamins. A lack of vitamin C, for example, will cause an illness called **scurvy**.

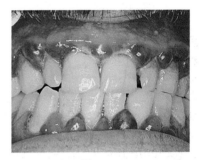

Figure 4 ▲ The symptoms of scurvy are bleeding gums and flaky skin

Ideas and Evidence

Scurvy is a disease with some gruesome symptoms. A person suffering from this illness will have bleeding gums and flaky skin. If left unchecked, scurvy could prove fatal. Up until the 18th Century, many sailors died on long voyages simply because of the lack of vitamin C in their diet. A British doctor found a simple cure: a daily ration of lime juice would prevent this appalling illness. British sailors got the nickname 'limey' from this practice. In fact all citrus fruits (oranges, grapefruits etc.) contain vitamin C, so it's lucky that we're not referred to today as 'lemons'! You can find out more about food and vitamins at http://www.dole5aday.com.

How does vitamin C help prevent scurvy?

Vitamin C helps make the 'glue' that holds our cells together. It is, therefore, important in the healing of cuts, wounds and burns. If we don't eat enough vitamin C, the 'glue' between our cells loses its strength and can make us bleed easily, resulting in scurvy. Some doctors now believe that vitamin C may also help in preventing certain types of cancer.

Minerals

Minerals are simple chemical elements, which our bodies need in very small amounts. They carry out important jobs in the body. For example, iron is used to make red blood cells, calcium is used to make bones and teeth, and sodium is used to help your muscles and nerves work.

A lack of these important minerals can cause very serious health problems. If you do not eat enough calcium, for example, your bones and teeth can be badly damaged. Osteoporosis is a disease in which bones become very fragile and are likely to break. It can often be prevented by eating a balanced diet rich in calcium and vitamin D, which helps the body to absorb the calcium.

Minerals are found in all types of food but certain minerals, such as iron, are more easily obtained from meat than from vegetables. This means that vegetarians need to eat lots of green vegetables to make sure they get enough iron from their food.

Fibre

This is made of cellulose from the cell walls of any plants that you eat. Your body cannot get energy from fibre; we can't break it down. However, it's important because it helps your intestines grip onto the food you've eaten and move it along. All the fibre you take into your body comes out of your body practically unchanged, but there is some evidence to suggest that eating fibre prevents stomach and intestinal cancers.

Water

Water is an essential part of your diet. You don't get any energy from water, but without it, humans die very quickly. Around 70% of your body is made up of water. The cytoplasm of your cells consists largely of water and your blood carries food and other materials around in a liquid called plasma which is mainly water.

Food tests

There are some simple chemical tests that you can perform on different foods to see if they contain proteins, fats, and the carbohydrates, starch and glucose.

1 The test for protein

Mix the food sample with a small amount of water in a test tube and shake it thoroughly. Add a few drops of Biuret A solution (dilute sodium hydroxide) followed by a few drops of Biuret B solution (dilute copper sulphate). If there is protein in the food, the solution will turn purple.

Figure 5 ▲   Testing for proteins

2 The test for fat

Mix the food sample with about half a test tube full of ethanol. Put a bung in the test tube and shake it thoroughly. Filter the mixture into a second clean test tube and then add some clean water. If fats are present in the food, a white emulsion is formed.

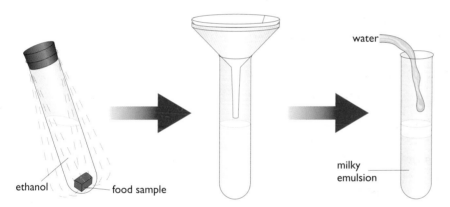

ethanol   food sample

water

milky emulsion

Figure 6 ▲   Testing for fats

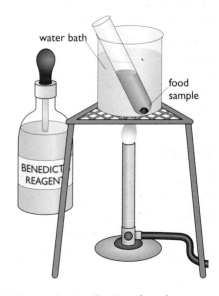

Figure 7 ▲   Testing for starch

3 The test for starch

Add a few drops of iodine solution to your food sample. If starch is present in the food, the iodine will change from a reddish-brown colour to a blue-black colour.

4 The test for glucose

Mix the food sample with some water in a test tube. Add to this a few drops of blue Benedict's reagent (copper (II) sulphate solution). Put the test tube in a water bath and heat gently. If there is glucose in the food, the solution will change colour from blue to green to brick red (depending on the amount of glucose present).

Note: Benedict's reagent only tests for glucose and other simple sugars found in fruits. It doesn't work with sucrose, the kind of sugar you put in tea.

water bath

food sample

BENEDICT REAGENT

Figure 8 ▲   Testing for glucose

Test Yourself

1   What are the functions of: a) protein, b) carbohydrate and c) fat in the body?

2   Using the information above, make a table to show which foods contain a lot of protein, carbohydrates and fats.

3   **a)** What kinds of food contain vitamins?
    b) Why are vitamins important?
    c) What is the effect of too little vitamin C in the diet?

4   What do you think will be the effect of eating too little calcium in your diet?

(a) fish and chips

(b) burger in a bun with salad

5   **a)** Which of the two meals shown above are 'balanced'.
    b) What is the effect of eating too much fat in your diet?

You are what you eat!

It seems strange to think that the piece of chicken or portion of baked beans that you ate yesterday will become a part of your hair, muscles, bones and teeth! Human beings use other living things (which we call food) as the raw materials for building their own bodies and fuelling their activities. Before we can do this, however, we have to break this food down into tiny little bits so that we can absorb it into our bloodstream. The scientific term for breaking food down is **digestion**. We do this using special chemical 'scissors' called **enzymes** inside a tube called the **alimentary canal**. This tube starts at your mouth, runs through your body and ends at your anus.

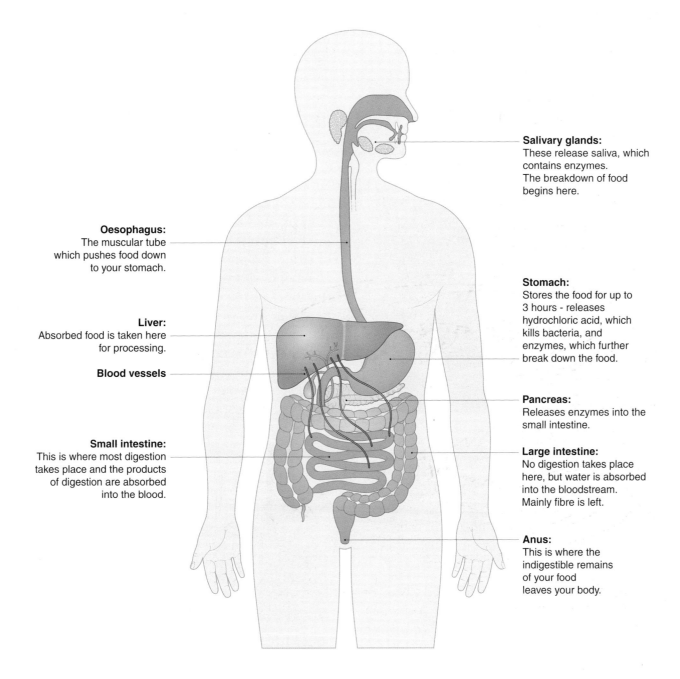

Salivary glands:
These release saliva, which contains enzymes. The breakdown of food begins here.

Oesophagus:
The muscular tube which pushes food down to your stomach.

Stomach:
Stores the food for up to 3 hours - releases hydrochloric acid, which kills bacteria, and enzymes, which further break down the food.

Liver:
Absorbed food is taken here for processing.

Blood vessels

Pancreas:
Releases enzymes into the small intestine.

Small intestine:
This is where most digestion takes place and the products of digestion are absorbed into the blood.

Large intestine:
No digestion takes place here, but water is absorbed into the bloodstream. Mainly fibre is left.

Anus:
This is where the indigestible remains of your food leaves your body.

Figure 9 ▲ The human digestive system

Test Yourself

6 Name three organs that release enzymes onto the food you've eaten.

7 What happens to any bacteria taken in with your food?

8 Where are the products of digestion absorbed?

9 List in order the parts of your body that food must pass through on its journey through the alimentary canal. Say what happens at each part that you mention.

Why does your body need digestive enzymes?

The story of Dr William Beaumont and Alexis St Martin

Dr William Beaumont

Dr Beaumont saw that he had a unique opportunity to investigate the effect that the stomach had on different kinds of food. His method involved tying bits of food onto pieces of string, dropping them into the hole and observing what happened to them. He noticed that beef, chicken, pork and cheese became mushy in the stomach juices, but that cabbage or root vegetables like carrots stayed unchanged. Alexis understandably became irritated by these experiments. Dr Beaumont noticed that a bad mood slowed down the process of digestion!

William Beaumont was a doctor who lived in America at the beginning of the 19th Century. He worked as an army doctor for many years, coping with many horrific injuries of war, sometimes having to amputate limbs without anaesthetic in hospital tents.

One day a Canadian fur trader called Alexis St Martin was shot in the stomach. Dr Beaumont wrote that this caused a wound "more than the size of a man's hand". Alexis survived the injury but the hole into his stomach never completely healed. This must have been very annoying because after eating or drinking, Alexis would have to cover the hole to stop the food and drink from falling out!

Test Yourself

10 How did Alexis' injury affect his everyday life?

11 What effect did the stomach have on a) meat and b) vegetables?

Most of the food that you take into your body is insoluble in water. Potatoes, for example, do not dissolve in boiling water. In order to be of any use to your body, the food that you absorb into your blood from your small intestine must be made soluble. Some of the foods that you eat, for example glucose and minerals, are already soluble and can simply pass directly into the bloodstream through the walls of the small intestine. Digestive enzymes speed up the breakdown of large insoluble food molecules into tiny, water soluble molecules. Some foods like white bread can be fully digested within two minutes of entering the small intestine.

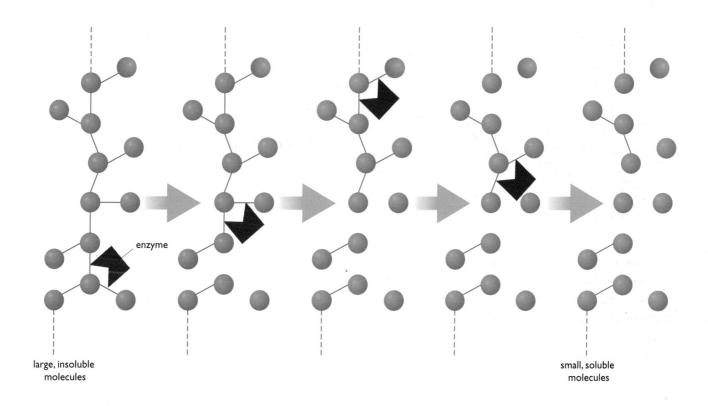

enzyme

large, insoluble molecules

small, soluble molecules

Figure 10 ▲   How an enzyme breaks down a large molecule

The small intestine – a kind of sponge!

To the naked eye, the walls of your small intestine appear fairly smooth, however, there are in fact tiny holes through which the products of digestion pass into the bloodstream. The products of digestion are taken to the liver from where they are carried around your body by the blood, and the tissues of your body then use them for energy (carbohydrates and fat) and to build more cells (protein). Your small intestine is very efficient at absorbing these molecules, partly because it is so long. In the average adult between 7 and 9 m of small intestine is coiled and packaged in the abdomen. This ensures that there is a large surface area for absorption of food particles.

Test Yourself

12 Give two reasons why your food needs to be broken down in digestion?

13 What's the advantage of having such a long small intestine?

14 Which organ first receives the food absorbed from your small intestine?

15 What happens in your large intestine?

Summary

When you have finished studying this chapter, you should understand that:

✔ A balanced diet contains all of the seven different food types: proteins, carbohydrates, fats, vitamins, minerals, fibre and water.

✔ How the seven food types are used by the body.

✔ The food we eat must be broken down by chemicals called enzymes before it can pass through the small intestine into the bloodstream.

End-of-Chapter Questions

1 Explain in your own words the following key terms you have met in this chapter:

protein

carbohydrate

fat

obesity

vitamins

scurvy

enzymes

alimentary canal

pancreas

small intestine

large intestine

absorption

2 Write a creative short story describing what happened to your breakfast. Imagine that **you are** your breakfast! (Include as much detail from Figure 9 as you can.)

End-of-Chapter Questions continued

3 Megan decided that she could investigate the amount of energy in different foods by burning them and using them to heat a test tube half filled with water. These are her results:

Food	Temperature increase °C
crisps	24
cheese	35
dried carrot	8
chicken	12

a) What steps should Megan take to ensure that she carries out a fair test?

b) Make a bar chart to present Megan's results.

c) i) Which food contains the highest amount of energy?

ii) What food type do you think it mostly contains?

d) Write a plan, using any laboratory equipment you like, to improve the method shown in the diagram above.

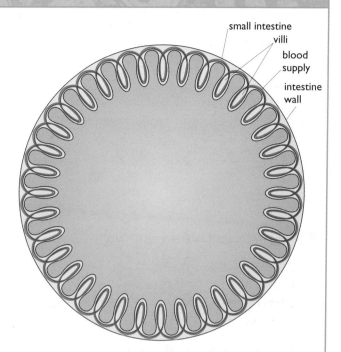

small intestine
villi
blood supply
intestine wall

4 Look at the diagram above. It shows the internal surface of the small intestine. Explain why you think it has these folds called villi.

5 Organic foods are those which are grown without using artificial pesticides or fertilisers. Some people say that they are healthier, others argue that they're no different to normally produced crops. Do some research to find out what the arguments are on both sides of the debate.

Fit and healthy

In April 1999, the American runner Maurice Greene set a new world record for the 100 m sprint, covering the distance in an amazing 9.79 seconds. His top speed, measured at the 60 m mark was more than 27 mph! It's pretty obvious when looking at the photograph what enabled Greene to run so fast – extremely strong leg muscles. In this chapter we will learn more about how muscles and joints work, and how important exercise is for a healthy life.

Muscle tissue

All types of movement (even getting goose pimples) are brought about by the action of **muscles**. Muscles are made up of special cells that can **contract** (get shorter) when told to by your brain.

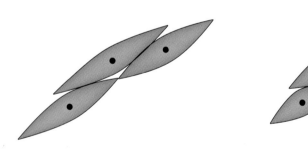

a) Muscle cells when relaxed   b) Muscle cells when contracted

Figure 1 ▲

Muscles are attached to your skeleton by thick, elastic tissues called **tendons**. You can feel tendons behind your knee and at the back of your heel. Tendons allow your muscles to pull on a bone. Muscles can't push, they can only pull. Muscles often work together in pairs. These are known as **antagonistic muscle pairs**.

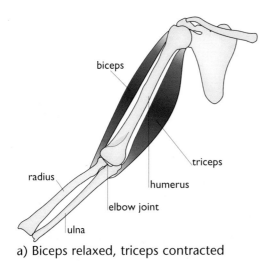

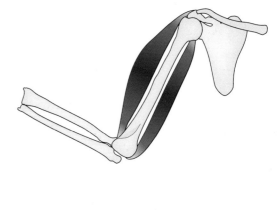

a) Biceps relaxed, triceps contracted

b) Biceps contracted, triceps relaxed

Figure 2 ▲

Look at Figure 2 and you'll see that the antagonistic pairs in your upper arm are called biceps and triceps muscles. When your biceps muscle contracts and your triceps muscle **relaxes** your lower arm is pulled upwards and your arm bends. To straighten your arm, your biceps muscle relaxes and your triceps muscle contracts, pulling your arm straight.

Test Yourself

1 Name the two muscles in your upper arm.

2 Fill in the gaps:

Muscles work by _____ which means getting shorter. They are attached to bones in your skeleton by _____ . Muscles can only _____ , they cannot _____ .

3 What does the term 'antagonistic muscle pair' mean?

4 Describe what happens to the muscles in your upper arm when a) you bend your arm and b) you straighten your arm.

Joints

A joint is the place where two bones meet. Your elbow is quite a simple type of joint known as a **hinge joint**. This type of joint only allows bending movements. Try to rotate the bottom of your arm independently of the top – you can't do it. Your hip and shoulder joints however, can be moved in all kinds of directions. Both of these are **ball and socket joints**.

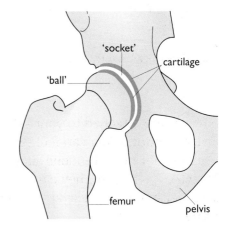

Figure 3 ▲ The hip joint. Ball and socket joints like this allow a greater range of movement than hinge joints.

37

The **cartilage** between your joints has two functions:

1 it acts as a kind of shock absorber between your bones
2 it provides an extremely smooth surface so your bones can glide over each other with the minimum of friction.

Like the rest of your body, joints can heal themselves, however overuse of any joint can lead to damage to the cartilage. Overuse of a joint for many years can result in a condition known as **osteoarthritis**. This is a painful condition which can restrict peoples' lives by severely reducing their mobility. Fortunately some patients can improve the quality of their life by having an operation to give them an artificial joint.

The damaged part of the joint is cut away and an artificial joint made of titanium, a strong metal, is cemented into the femur. The new joint works well for many years, but it does wear and sometimes the cement fails, allowing the new joint to become loose.

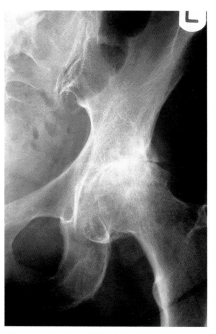

Figure 4 ▲ This hip joint has been damaged by osteoarthritis

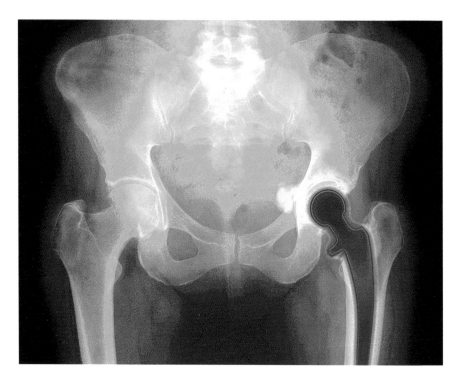

Figure 5 ◄ An artificial hip joint in place in the body

Test Yourself

5 What kind of joints exist at: a) your knee, b) your shoulder and c) your elbow?

6 What is the function of the cartilage in your joints?

7 What is osteoarthritis?

8 What kind of material do you think would make the best replacement hip joint? Explain your answer.

Exercise and health

Apart from eating a balanced diet, taking regular exercise is probably the most important thing you can do to stay healthy. As well as being great fun, regular exercise:

- reduces the chance of dying from heart disease
- reduces the chance of developing diabetes
- reduces the risk of developing high blood pressure and helps reduce blood pressure in people who already have high blood pressure
- reduces the chance of developing cancer of the colon
- reduces feelings of depression and anxiety
- helps control weight
- helps build and maintain healthy bones, muscles and joints
- helps older adults become stronger and better able to move about without falling.

For exercise to be of most benefit to your health it has to:

- be regular: at least three times a week
- raise your heart rate for 15 minutes or more: the longer your heart rate is raised, the better the activity (up to a point!)
- be something you enjoy.

Test Yourself

9 Rank the following sports in order of health benefit:

   Cricket, training to run a half marathon, 100 m sprint, darts, hockey, bowls, hill walking.

10 List the three benefits of exercise that you consider to be the most important. Explain your choices.

11 Can you think of any sports that would have little health benefits? List them and explain your answers.

Summary

When you have finished studying this chapter, you should understand that:

✔ All types of movement are brought about by the action of muscles.

✔ Muscles work across joints and are attached to bones by tendons.

✔ Muscles contract and relax to cause movement.

✔ Muscles can't push, they can only pull, so for a joint to be able to bend and straighten, two muscles are needed. These are called antagonistic muscle pairs. An

example is the biceps and tricpes muscles that work the elbow joint.

✔ There are two types of joint: hinge joints and ball and socket joints. Hinge joints only allow bending, while ball and socket joints allow a whole range of movements.

✔ Overuse of joints can lead to a painful condition called osteoarthritis.

✔ Taking regular exercise is essential to maintain health.

End-of-Chapter Questions

1 Explain in your own words the following key terms you have met in this chapter:

muscle

contraction

tendons

antagonistic muscle pairs

relaxation

hinge joint

ball and socket joint

cartilage

osteoarthritis

2

Jim wanted to find out the effect of regular exercise upon his muscles. He trained his biceps muscles three times a week by lifting dumbells as shown in the diagram opposite.

He tested himself to find out the maximum weight that he could lift at the end of each week. Here's a table of his results:

Week number	Maximum weight/kg
1	5
2	8
3	9
4	5
5	10

a) Plot a graph to present the above data.

b) What effect did regular weightlifting have on Jim's biceps muscles?

c) What should Jim have done to ensure that this was a fair test?

d) What type of exercise could Jim do if he wanted to test his triceps muscle?

End-of-Chapter Questions continued

3 Your friend Ling is exercise mad! She runs every day, plays hockey and football for school teams, and does street skateboarding in the evenings. Now and again, she complains of knee pains.

a) What damage might she be doing to her joints?

b) Write a note to her, explaining why exercise is really good for you, and why it's also important to give your joints a rest.

4 The table below shows the world record times (1996) for different running events:

Distance/m	Men	Women
100	9.85	10.49
200	19.72	21.34
400	43.29	47.60
800	1:41.73	1:53.28
1500	3:27.37	3:50.46
3000	7:25.11	8:08.11
5000	12:44.39	14:36.45
10 000	26:43.53	29:31.78

a) Make a table in your book which shows the average speeds that these athletes ran. Use the equation:
Average speed = Distance (m) / Time (s)

b) Plot a line graph showing the average speed at each different distance.

c) For each distance calculate the percentage difference in average speed between men and women.

d) What trends do you notice? Attempt to explain them.

5 Reproduction

All living things reproduce. Simple organisms such as bacteria or yeast simply get bigger and then divide into two new daughter cells.

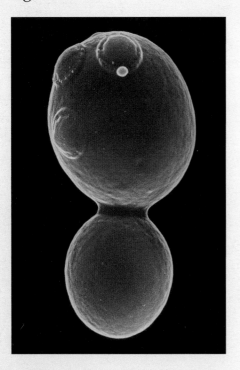

This kind of reproduction is known as **asexual reproduction** ('a' means without) and produces offspring which are identical to each other and to the parent. These are known as **clones**.

More complex organisms, like humans, produce offspring by **sexual reproduction**. This involves the **fusion** (joining) of sex cells (**gametes**). The male gamete is the **sperm**, the female gamete is the **egg**. This kind of reproduction produces offspring with some of the characteristics of both parents. In this chapter we will explore the process of fertilisation in humans and learn how the foetus develops.

External fertilisation

In many aquatic animals, gametes are simply released into the water and meet each other by chance. Many types of invertebrates, fish and amphibians rely on this type of **external fertilisation**. To be effective, millions of gametes must be produced and released at the same time.

The sea urchin in Figure 1 produces millions of gametes and simply releases them into the sea. Inevitably some sperm cells bump into some egg cells and when this happens, the sperm fertilise the eggs which then divide and eventually grow into adult urchins. Many millions of eggs remain unfertilised, but because of the sheer numbers released, enough are fertilised to ensure the survival of the species.

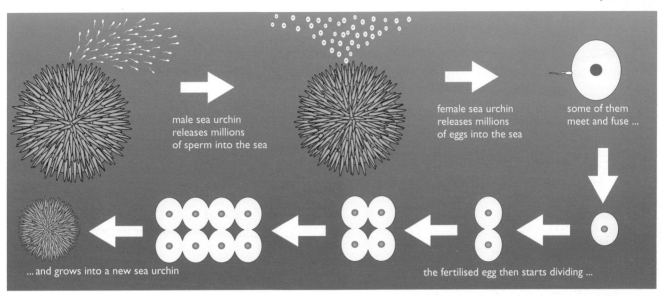

Figure 1 ▲ The lifecycle of a sea urchin

The male stickleback tries to reduce the inefficiency of this process by building a 'nest' of weeds around his mate. The female fish releases thousands of eggs into this nest and the male then releases sperm onto them.

Frogs reproduce in ponds during late winter or early spring. The males grab onto the backs of females in an embrace known as an amplexus and release sperm onto the eggs as they emerge from the female's body. The fertilised eggs develop into tadpoles which eventually change into frogs.

Figure 2 ► These frogs are in amplexus

Test Yourself

1 Describe how bacteria reproduce.

2 What are the differences between sexual and asexual reproduction?

3 Explain what is meant by the term 'gamete'?

4 Why do you think that frogs only produce hundreds of eggs at a time whereas sea urchins must produce millions if they are to reproduce effectively?

Internal fertilisation

In mammals, birds and reptiles, a different, more efficient form of reproduction is used. The sperm and egg meet each other inside the female's reproductive system. This is known as **internal fertilisation**. Humans are, of course, mammals and the following section is a description of how human beings reproduce.

The male reproductive system

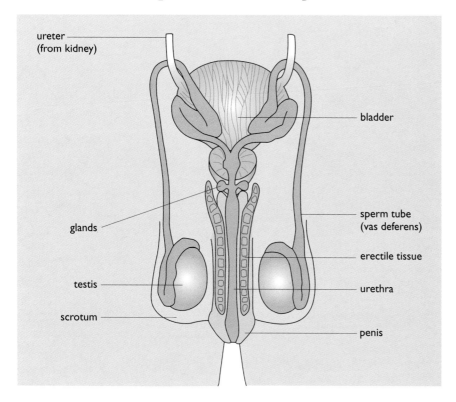

Figure 3 ◄ The male reproductive system

Millions of sperm cells are made in the **testes** of males every day from the onset of puberty until the day they die. These delicate organs are situated in the scrotum outside of the body so that the testes are 2°C cooler than the rest of your body. They work best at this temperature. The sperm are then transported to the epididymis where they are stored. The **prostate gland** produces a nutritive, milky liquid. The mixture of the sperm and milky liquid is known as **semen**.

Test Yourself

5   Starting in the testes, trace the route that the sperm has to take on its journey to the outside world.

6   Why is it important that the testes lie outside of the body?

7   What happens in the prostate gland?

The female reproductive system

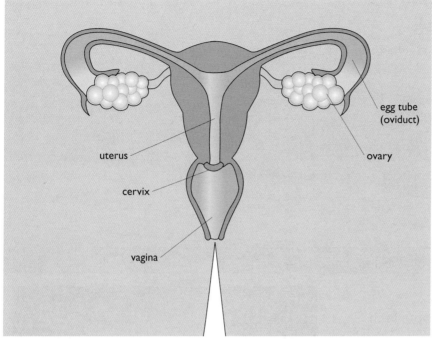

Figure 4 ◄ The female reproductive system

uterus

cervix

vagina

egg tube (oviduct)

ovary

Make a triangle with the thumbs and forefingers of both hands. This is approximately how much space the whole of the female reproductive system takes up. In contrast to men, all the eggs that a woman ever has are made in her **ovaries** before she is born! Between the ages of 11–14, a woman begins to release an egg from either of her ovaries into an egg tube (**oviduct**) every month until the age of about 45, when egg release stops (this is called the **menopause**). The egg is then wafted slowly down the oviduct by special cells called ciliated epithelium cells (cilia). Fertilisation only takes place if a sperm meets an egg in this tube.

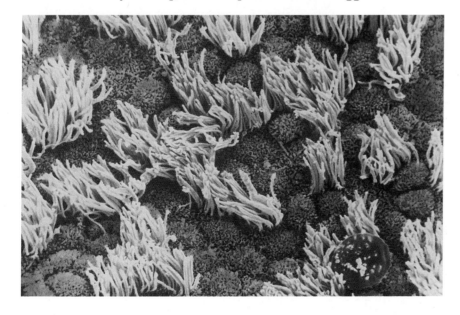

Figure 5 ◄ These ciliated cells are responsible for wafting the egg cell from the ovary down the oviduct

Test Yourself

8   Where are egg cells produced?

9   How often are egg cells released?

10   Starting in the ovaries, trace the route that the egg has to take on its journey to the outside world.

11   Which structures inside the oviduct move the egg along towards the uterus?

12   Where does fertilisation take place?

13   Make a table listing the features of the male and female reproductive systems.

Extension box

Sperm and egg cells

In Chapter 2 we saw how well adapted the sperm cells and egg cells are to carry out their roles in fertilisation. Sperm cells have a long tail and a streamlined shape to enable them to swim through the female's body to the egg cell. The egg cell itself is very much larger than the sperm cell, as you can see from the photo. This is because the egg has been designed to contain enough stored food to maintain the developing embryo after fertilisation until it can start receiving nutrition from the mother.

There is also an enormous difference in the numbers of sperm and eggs produced. Millions of sperm are made every day, but a female is born with all the eggs she will ever need – around 2 million. The reason for this difference is that because the sperm have such a long journey and many of them don't make it, millions of sperm have to be released to maximise the chance of at least one sperm successfully reaching the egg.

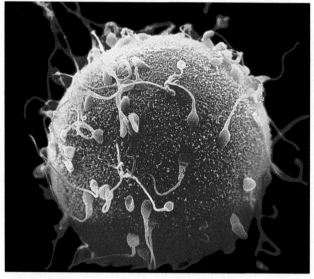

Figure 6 ▲   The egg is hundreds of times larger than the sperm

Making a baby

Having a baby is the most life-changing event that will ever happen to a couple. Babies are extremely dependent upon their parents for a long time. In the first few months their sleeping patterns are erratic (as you will know if you have a younger brother or sister) and they are completely helpless. Being a parent is very difficult, expensive and often stressful. When to have a baby is a decision which most couples consider very seriously indeed!

Sexual intercourse

A sperm cell and an egg cell must meet inside an oviduct if fertilisation is to take place. In order for this to happen, human beings have sexual intercourse. This is a pleasurable part of a loving relationship and is often known as 'making love'. When a couple are ready to make love, sexual excitement makes the man's **penis** become stiffer, harder and longer. This happens because the erectile tissue in his penis fills with blood. When a woman becomes sexually excited, special glands inside her **vagina** make a lubricating fluid which makes it easier for the man to put his penis inside her vagina. The man and woman move their hips backwards and forwards increasing the pleasurable sensations that they both get. Eventually, semen (which contains millions of sperm cells) is released into the vagina.

Figure 7 ▼ A couple having sexual intercourse

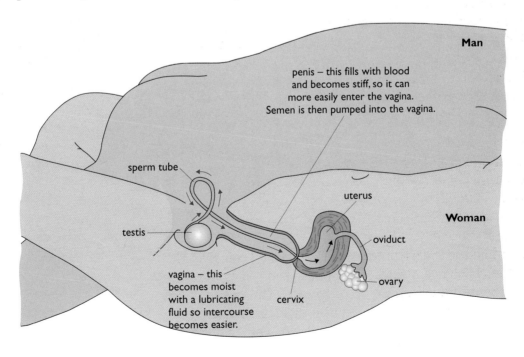

47

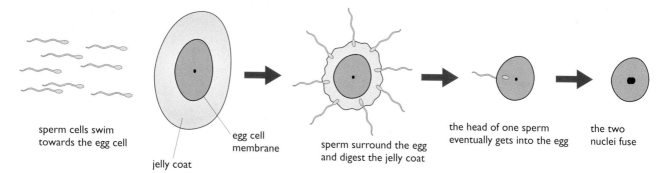

sperm cells swim
towards the egg cell

jelly coat

egg cell
membrane

sperm surround the egg
and digest the jelly coat

the head of one sperm
eventually gets into the egg

the two
nuclei fuse

These sperm now have to swim a huge distance to get to the oviduct and the egg. It takes about 10 hours of constant swimming to reach the oviduct. If you scale things up, it's equivalent to a human being having to cross the Atlantic Ocean! Many millions of sperm die during the journey. Only the strongest swimmers actually get to the egg. The first sperm to get to the egg pushes its way through the cell membrane and immediately loses its tail.

If you look at Figure 8, you'll see that the nuclei of the sperm and egg join together making a new cell. This is the first cell of a new human being and is known as a **zygote**. The zygote will travel down the oviduct to the uterus, where it implants itself and eventually grows into a baby.

Figure 8 ▲ Millions of sperm swim towards the egg, but only one can fertilise it

Test Yourself

14 List in order the parts of a woman's body that a sperm must pass through on its journey to the egg cell.

15 Describe what happens when a sperm meets an egg.

16 Why do you think an egg is so much bigger than a sperm cell?

17 What is a zygote?

Pregnancy

After fertilisation, the zygote produces more cells by cell division. Every 20 hours, each cell divides into two so that 4 days after fertilisation, the **embryo** is made up of 16 cells. The zygote becomes known as an embryo as soon as it divides. Amazingly, just two days later you can see that the embryo is being organised into some kind of structure.

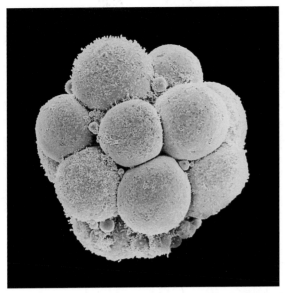

Figure 9 ▲ At four days old, the embryo still looks like a ball of cells. Length = 0.15 mm

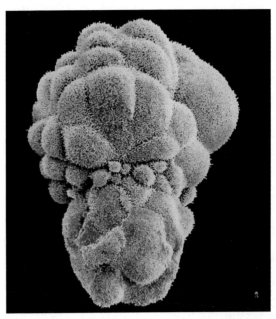

Figure 10 ▲ At six days old, the embryo has some structure. Length = 0.15 mm

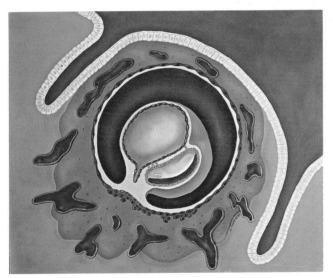

Figure 11 ▲ At 13 days old, the placenta begins to develop. Length = 0.2 mm

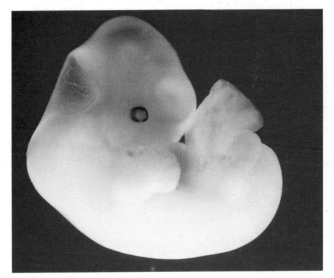

Figure 12 ▲ At 24 days old, the embryo's heart begins to beat. Length = 3 mm

The embryo secretes enzymes onto the wall of the uterus making a space so that it can attach itself, enabling it to get food and oxygen from the mother's bloodstream.

By day 13, the blood vessels of the embryo are beginning to develop and a new organ has started to grow from the embryo. This organ, called the **placenta**, is responsible for getting food and oxygen from the mother's blood supply.

By day 24, the embryo does not yet resemble a human being. It's head is obvious, but it hasn't got legs yet – just a tail! It's heart, however, has already started to beat.

By day 48, the embryo looks very much like a human being. At this stage, we call it a **foetus**. Its limbs, head, eyes and ears have begun to develop and the brain is beginning to function.

By the 16th week, all the organs are formed and the foetus can now move around. It may even start to suck its thumb!

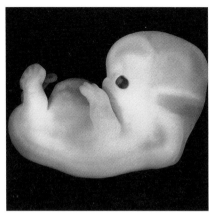

Figure 13 ▲ At 48 days old, most of the foetus' organs are formed, but they would not work outside the uterus. Length = 15 mm

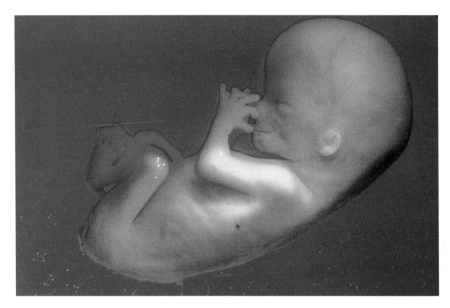

Figure 14 ◄ At 16 weeks, the foetus begins to move around and is big enough to make the woman look pregnant. Length = 20 cm

After 36 weeks of development, the foetus' head points downwards, ready to be born. He or she can now turn towards the light and can hear quite well. Some people claim that babies are able to recognise their mother's voice as soon as they're born!

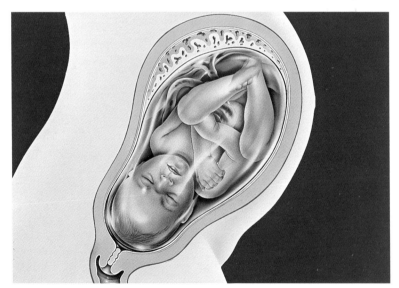

Figure 15 ▲ At 36 weeks, the baby is filling all available space inside the uterus and the mother may have difficulty getting around. The baby is normally born 4 weeks later. Length = 46 cm

Once the baby has been born, it is able to suck milk from its mother's breast. For the first three months of its life, this is all the nutrition that it needs.

Figure 16 ▲ This baby is receiving food from its mother's breast.

18 Make a timeline to illustrate the development of the embryo from fertilisation to birth, 40 weeks later.

19 Construct a line graph to show how the embryo changes in length from fertilisation to week 36.

Inside the uterus

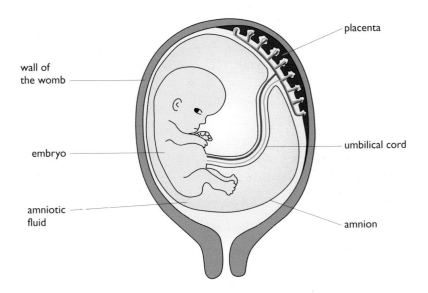

wall of
the womb

embryo

amniotic
fluid

placenta

umbilical cord

amnion

Figure 17 ◄ A 24-week-old foetus inside its mother's uterus

Figure 17 shows a 24-week-old foetus inside the uterus. Like all living things it needs food, water, oxygen and to be able to get rid of its waste. The organ responsible for these functions is the placenta. This large disc-shaped organ is able to absorb food and oxygen directly from the mother's bloodstream. These are then passed to the foetus through blood vessels in the **umbilical cord**. Just like you, the foetus produces a toxic gas called carbon dioxide as it respires. However, it doesn't get rid of it by breathing out, instead the placenta passes it to the mother's bloodstream and the mother breathes it out! The placenta is also responsible for protecting the foetus from harmful substances. Some substances, such as alcohol and certain drugs, can actually pass through the placenta into the foetus and can affect the way that the foetus grows.

If you look carefully at Figure 17 you'll see that the foetus is floating in some liquid called **amniotic fluid** which is contained by a sac called the **amnion**. The baby itself makes amniotic fluid by urinating into the amnion. Floating in this fluid protects the baby from jolts and bumps.

Birth

After 40 weeks of growth inside the uterus, the baby is ready to be born. Throughout her pregnancy, the mother's uterus will have been practising for this moment by making small contractions to tone the muscles of the uterus. But the contractions that the mother now feels will be much stronger. As these contractions become stronger, the cervix begins to open so that the baby's head can fit through it into the vagina. After a huge and exhausting muscular effort from the mother, the baby will finally be pushed out of the mother's body into the outside world where it will take its first breath.

One of the first things that the midwife will do when the baby is born is to cut the umbilical cord which connects the baby to the placenta. The placenta comes out of the uterus after the baby and is known as the afterbirth. The baby now needs to get food itself by sucking milk from its mother's breasts. This milk is extremely important to the survival of the baby as it not only contains all the nutrients the baby needs, but it also contains antibodies from the mother (see Chapter 8) which help protect the newborn baby from infection in its first few months of life.

Test Yourself

20 How does a foetus get oxygen and food while inside the uterus?

21 How does a foetus get rid of the waste created during respiration?

22 What is amniotic fluid and why is it useful?

23 Why does the uterus make 'practice contractions' throughout the mother's pregnancy?

24 Describe in your own words what happens when a mother gives birth.

Growing up

The most obvious effect of growing up is increasing in size. Both boys and girls seem to do this at the same rate and don't actually look that different until they hit **puberty**. Before we explore the details, take this mini quiz to see how much you already know.

Puberty quiz

1 Girls normally start puberty between which ages?
a) 13–16
b) 10–12
c) 8–13
d) 16–20

2 Boys normally start puberty between which ages?
a) 8–12
b) 15–16
c) 10–15
d) 16–19

3 On the whole, boys suffer more from acne than girls do. True or False?

4 It's normal for girls to put on a certain amount of fat during puberty. True or False?

5 How much blood does a woman usually lose during her monthly period?
a) A teaspoon
b) A quarter of a cup
c) A pint
d) A litre

6 A wet dream means
a) a boy's eyesight will now start to deteriorate
b) a boy probably had a sexual dream
c) a boy's acne will get worse

7 Some women experience mood swings around the time of their period. True or False?

8 Acne is caused by a lack of personal hygiene. True or False?

9 The armpits of both men and women start to smell more during puberty. True or False?

10 At what age do girls (on average) stop getting taller?
a) 20
b) 18
c) 16
d) 14

11 At what age do boys (on average) stop getting taller?
a) 21
b) 19
c) 18
d) 16

Answers: 1 – c, 2 – c, 3 – True, 4 – True, 5 – b, 6 – b, 7 – True, 8 – False, 9 – True, 10 – c 11 – c

Puberty

Everyone is unique, which means that your body will go through puberty according to its own timetable. Puberty marks the time at which a child's body starts turning into an adult's body. These changes are under the control of chemicals called **hormones**. These are produced by your brain and sex organs. If you are male, your testes produce a hormone called **testosterone**. This hormone makes your body develop masculine characteristics which are shown in Figure 18.

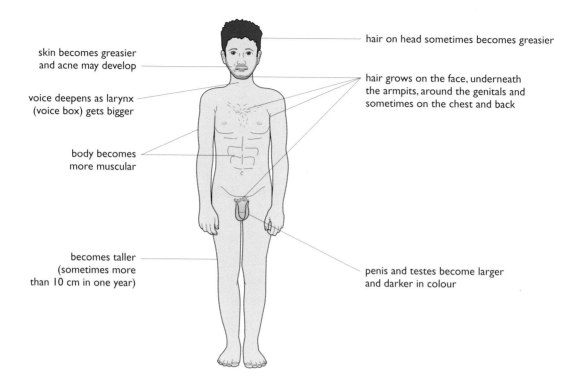

skin becomes greasier
and acne may develop

voice deepens as larynx
(voice box) gets bigger

body becomes
more muscular

becomes taller
(sometimes more
than 10 cm in one year)

hair on head sometimes becomes greasier

hair grows on the face, underneath
the armpits, around the genitals and
sometimes on the chest and back

penis and testes become larger
and darker in colour

If you are female, your ovaries produce two types of hormones –
progesterone and **oestrogen**. These hormones make your body
develop the female characteristics shown in Figure 19.

Figure 18 ▲ Male secondary sexual characteristics

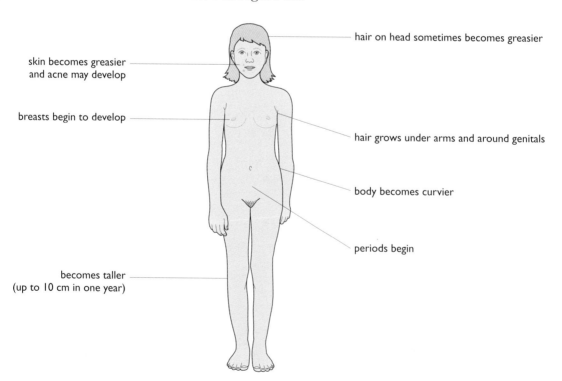

skin becomes greasier
and acne may develop

breasts begin to develop

becomes taller
(up to 10 cm in one year)

hair on head sometimes becomes greasier

hair grows under arms and around genitals

body becomes curvier

periods begin

In addition to physical changes, boys and girls experience
complex emotional changes. In fact adolescence is often
described as an emotional rollercoaster ride!

Figure 19 ▲ Female secondary sexual characteristics

25 Write down all the changes that happen to both girls and boys during puberty.

26 Write down the changes that only happen to boys.

27 Write down the changes that only happen to girls.

28 What is a hormone?

The monthly cycle – menstruation

A girl's monthly period is controlled by a complex series of hormonal changes inside her body. These hormones control the release of an egg from one of the ovaries every month. The uterus prepares itself to receive a fertilised egg. If it does, then any further egg release for the next nine months is halted and pregnancy occurs. If the egg is not fertilised, then the uterus lining breaks down (which causes blood loss) and leaves the body together with the unfertilised egg through the vagina. This is known as **menstruation** (the period) and lasts between 4 and 7 days. After the period, the uterus lining starts to rebuild itself to prepare for another possible pregnancy. The whole cycle takes around 28 days.

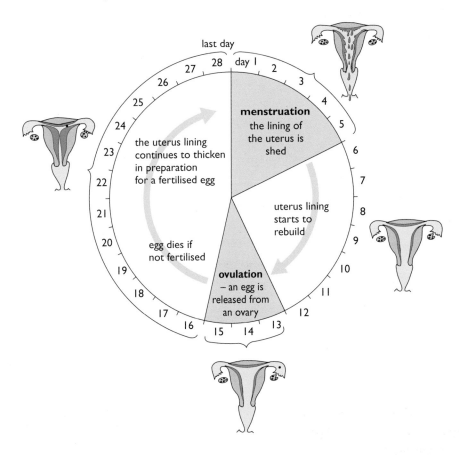

Figure 20 ◄ The menstrual cycle

Test Yourself

29 How often is an egg released from an ovary?

30 On which day of the menstrual cycle is an egg released?

31 What happens to the egg if fertilisation doesn't occur?

32 What is menstruation?

33 A sperm can live on average for around 2 days. An egg can only be fertilised up until 2 days after it has been released. On which days of the monthly cycle should a couple have sexual intercourse to maximise their chances of pregnancy?

Summary

When you have finished studying this chapter, you should understand that:

✔ Asexual reproduction happens in simple organisms and produces clones.

✔ More complex organisms reproduce sexually by fusion of a sperm and an egg.

✔ The sperm and egg cell (the gametes) contain the characteristics of the father and mother, respectively. The offspring formed by fertilisation of these cells has characteristics from both parents.

✔ Some aquatic animals carry out external fertilisation.

✔ In mammals, birds and reptiles, fertilisation occurs inside the female's body. This is known as internal fertilisation.

✔ Males produce sperm cells in their testes. Millions of sperm are produced every day.

✔ Females are born with all the eggs they will ever need. One egg is released every month from the ovaries.

✔ Sexual intercourse enables the sperm and egg cells to come together and fuse. The resulting zygote develops into a baby.

✔ The developing foetus is dependent on the mother for food and oxygen.

✔ All boys and girls pass through a stage called puberty, during which time their bodies undergo numerous changes. Puberty is controlled by chemicals called hormones.

✔ From puberty, females have a monthly cycle, during which the body prepares itself for pregnancy. If pregnancy does not occur, the uterus lining is shed in a process called menstruation.

End-of-Chapter Questions

1 Explain in your own words the following key terms you have met in this chapter:

asexual reproduction

clone

sexual reproduction

fusion

sperm

egg

gamete

external fertilisation

internal fertilisation

testes

prostate gland

semen

ovaries

oviduct

menopause

penis

vagina

zygote

embryo

placenta

foetus

umbilical cord

amniotic fluid

amnion

puberty

hormones

testosterone

progesterone

oestrogen

menstruation

2 Which system of fertilisation do you think is the more efficient – internal or external fertilisation? Explain your answer.

3 The following table shows the height of a girl and a boy at different ages:

| Age | Height (cm) | |
	Girl	Boy
0	35	34
2	93	90
5	110	111
10	140	132
12	160	139
14	163	162
16	165	181
18	165	184

a) Plot a line graph to display the figures above.

b) Between which ages do i) girls and ii) boys experience a large growth spurt?

c) What is the name of the group of chemicals that cause this to happen?

4 Imagine you are a doctor speaking to a couple who are keen to start a family. What advice do you need to give them?

5 There are often physical reasons why some couples find it difficult to become pregnant. Some of these are listed below:

a) Cilia in oviduct do not function.

b) Oviducts are blocked.

c) Oestrogen and progesterone are not produced at the right time.

d) Man's sperm count is very low.

e) Man's sperm are attacked by his own immune system.

Explain why each of the above causes make it difficult for pregnancy to occur.

Breathing and respiration

The diver in the photograph has been training himself to dive for very long periods without the aid of an aqualung. The world record for free diving is 162 m, which was set by Francisco 'Pipin' Ferreras on 18th January 2000. To accomplish this remarkable feat, Francisco had to hold his breath for more than three minutes! Find out more about this fascinating extreme sport at: http://www.freediving.net.

Even though you don't give breathing a second thought, it's something that you'll do about 20 times a minute every day of your life.

Ideas and Evidence

Joseph Priestly and the discovery of oxygen

Figure 1 ▲ Joseph Priestly

Joseph Priestly was born near Leeds on 13 March 1733 . He was brought up by a very strict religious family and eventually became pastor of a small church in Leeds.

Up until he was 33 years old, he had no real interest in science, but this changed the day he met Benjamin Franklin, the famous scientist who flew a kite into a lightning storm to show that it contained electricity.

As a result of this meeting, Priestly became very interested in science and began to experiment with electricity and gases in the air around us. His most famous discovery was that living things need oxygen to stay alive. Priestly discovered that oxygen is made by green plants during photosynthesis and could also be made by heating a red powder called mercuric oxide. Below is an excerpt from Priestly's diary which describes an experiment he performed with a rather unfortunate mouse!

"On the 8th of this month I procured a mouse, and put it into a glass vessel, containing two ounce-measures of the air from mercuric oxide. Had it been common air, a full-grown mouse, as this was, would have lived in it about a quarter of an hour. In this air, however, my mouse lived a full hour; and though it was taken out seemingly dead, it appeared to have been only exceedingly chilled; for, upon being held to the fire, it presently revived, and appeared not to have received any harm from the experiment."

Test Yourself

1   What do you think that Priestly was trying to prove in this experiment?

2   Why do you think that the mouse appeared to be almost dead at the end of the experiment?

It might surprise you to find out that nitrogen is in fact the most abundant gas in the air that surrounds you, making up approximately 79% of the atmosphere. Oxygen only makes up about 20%. The rest of the atmosphere is made up of small quantities of carbon dioxide, hydrogen and other gases.

The breathing system

It was the Egyptian physician Ibn an Nafis who, in 1242, first noticed that blood travelled through the **lungs**. He wrote "the blood from the heart must flow through the pulmonary artery (one of the main blood vessels of the heart) to the lungs, spread through its substances and be mingled there with air". This was a key observation and one that hinted at the main job of the lungs, which is to get oxygen into the blood. Your lungs have another function which Nafis could not have known about: they also remove carbon dioxide, a toxic gas, from your blood.

Your lungs are situated in the upper half of your body – the **thorax**. They are connected to your nose and mouth by a tube called the windpipe or **trachea**, which itself branches into two tubes called **bronchi**. When you breathe in, air is sucked through your nose and mouth and travels through your trachea, bronchi and into your lungs. The insides of the lungs are not hollow. If you look at Figure 3, you'll see that each bronchus divides many times into tubes called **bronchioles**, which end up in tiny air sacs known as **alveoli**.

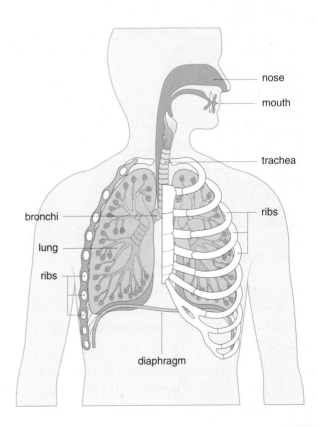

Figure 2 ▶ The structure of the breathing system

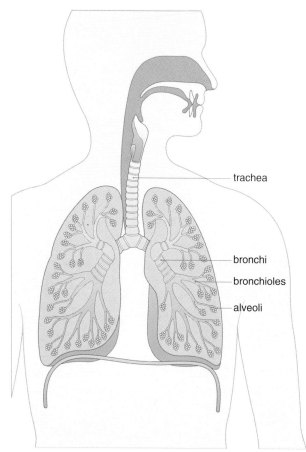

trachea

bronchi

bronchioles

alveoli

Figure 3 ▲ The internal structure of the lungs

Test Yourself

3 What is the scientific name for the upper part of your chest?

4 Copy and complete the sentences abut breathing below:

When you inhale, air is sucked in through your mouth and then travels through a tube called the _____, which divides to form _____.

These divide again to form tiny tubes called _____ which end in air sacs known as _____.

5 What are the two functions of the lungs?

Gas exchange

In the alveoli, oxygen **diffuses** (moves) from the inhaled air into the blood and carbon dioxide diffuses out of the blood into the air to be exhaled. This is called **gas exchange**. It can happen because:

- the walls of the alveoli are extremely thin
- there's only a very short distance for the gases to travel between the bloodstream and the air in the lungs
- the walls of the alveoli are moist, so oxygen can dissolve.

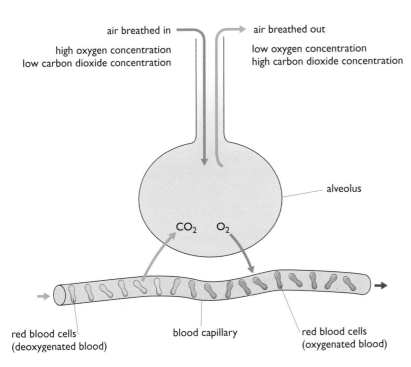

Figure 4 ◄ Exchange of oxygen
and carbon dioxide in an alveolus

air breathed in — high oxygen concentration low carbon dioxide concentration

air breathed out — low oxygen concentration high carbon dioxide concentration

alveolus

CO_2 O_2

red blood cells (deoxygenated blood)

blood capillary

red blood cells (oxygenated blood)

Your lungs contain thousands of alveoli. If they were all flattened and spread out, they would cover the same area as a tennis court! This large surface area means that your lungs are very good at getting a lot of oxygen into your blood and removing a large volume of carbon dioxide with each breath. The oxygen that diffuses into your bloodstream is captured by your red blood cells where it combines with a red pigment called **haemoglobin**. As your heart pumps, the red blood cells are circulated around the body releasing oxygen to the organs where it is needed for **respiration** (see page 63).

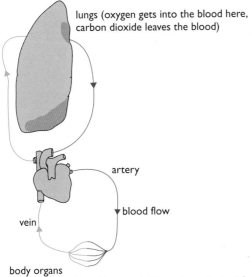

Figure 5 ◄ The structure of the circulatory system

lungs (oxygen gets into the blood here, carbon dioxide leaves the blood)

artery

blood flow

vein

body organs
(oxygen leaves blood here and diffuses in to the body's organs; carbon dioxide made as a result of respiration diffuses into the blood)

Test Yourself

6 List three features that make the lungs efficient at absorbing oxygen.

7 The table below shows the composition of gases in the air that you breathe in and out.

	% nitrogen	% oxygen	% carbon dioxide
Inhaled air	79	20	0.04
Exhaled air	79	16	4

a) Calculate the percentage of oxygen that your lungs absorb from the air. Use this formula:

$$\% \text{ oxygen absorbed} = \frac{\% \text{ oxygen inhaled}}{\% \text{ oxygen exhaled}} \times 100$$

b) What happens to the nitrogen that enters your lungs?

8 What is the function of haemoglobin?

9 How does your body ensure that oxygen gets to every organ?

Extension box

What makes you breathe in?

It's a weird thought, but the weight of the air pushing down on each of us is equivalent to about 1 ton! It's this weight that causes air to have **pressure**. We use this pressure to force air into our lungs, but to do this, we first need to decrease the pressure inside our thorax.

Figure 6 shows how your **diaphragm** and rib muscles act together to increase the volume of your thorax. The diaphragm is a muscular sheet which flattens when you breathe in. At the same time your rib muscles contract which forces your ribs upwards and outwards. These two changes increase the volume of your thorax considerably. This increase in volume causes a decrease in pressure inside your thorax and air from the outside pushes its way into your lungs until the pressure is equalised. Breathing out is the exact opposite of this process.

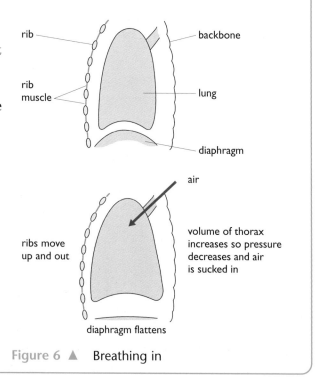

Figure 6 ▲ Breathing in

10 Name the two muscles that bring about breathing.

11 What do these muscles do to bring about a decrease in the pressure inside your thorax?

12 Make a flowchart to show what happens inside your thorax when you breathe out. Use this statement to begin:

Your rib muscles contract, forcing ⟶ your ribs downwards

Respiration

glucose

Figure 7 ◄ Glucose burns brightly in oxygen

The boy in Figure 7 is putting burning glucose into pure oxygen. As you can see, it releases large amounts of energy in the form of heat and light.

LIME WATER

Figure 8 ◄ The carbon dioxide from the burning glucose turns the lime water milky

If you look carefully at Figure 7, you'll see droplets of moisture being formed as the glucose burns and in Figure 8, the pupil has added some lime water to the gas jar which has become cloudy. Lime water becomes cloudy when mixed with carbon dioxide, so from this experiment we can see that burning glucose produces water and carbon dioxide.

Your body's favourite fuel is glucose and it gets its energy for all life processes by chemically 'burning' glucose in the cytoplasm of your cells. Once food has been digested and absorbed into your bloodstream, glucose circulates in your blood and is combined with oxygen in your body's cells. This results in a chemical reaction that releases energy in forms that your body can use. This process is known as respiration and can be summarised by the following word equation:

$$\text{glucose} + \text{oxygen} \longrightarrow \text{carbon dioxide} + \text{water} + \text{energy}$$

Breathing is often confused with respiration, but they're really two separate things. Breathing gets oxygen into your bloodstream and respiration is your body's way of releasing energy. Just like in the burning glucose experiment, respiration also produces water, which you can use, and carbon dioxide, which is toxic and must be removed by your lungs. The energy produced is needed for all your life processes.

For example:

- muscular contraction to allow movement
- keeping your body temperature at 37°C
- building your body up

Test Yourself

13 What does the term respiration mean?

14 Where does respiration take place?

15 Cover the word equation for respiration with your pencil case and try to write it down from memory.

16 Name three things that your body needs energy for.

Ideas and Evidence

On the 9th November 1992, Sir Ranulph Fiennes and Dr Mike Stroud set off on an expedition. Their remarkable goal was to cross the Antarctic, a journey of 2500 km across snow and ice without assistance. They carried a huge amount of food with them – enough for them to consume 22 000 kJ per day. That's more than double the amount of food recommended for an active adult male! Looking at the photos you'll see that when they returned they had both lost around about half of their body weight.

... After

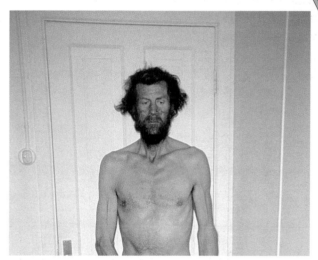

Before ...

Test Yourself

17 Ranulph Fiennes and Dr Mike Stroud walked 30 km each day pulling a sledge weighing 220 kg in temperatures as low as –50°C. Explain why they lost so much weight even though they ate a huge amount of food. (You must use your knowledge of respiration in your answer.)

18 Women are generally lighter than men, which means it takes less energy for them to move from one place to another. They also have slightly more body fat than men, which means they lose heat more slowly. Who do you think would make the better polar travellers, men or women? Explain your answer.

Summary

When you have finished studying this chapter, you should understand that:

✔ The lungs are responsible for getting oxygen into our body and removing the waste gas, carbon dioxide.

✔ Inhaled air passes from the mouth or nose down the trachea, into the bronchi, through the bronchioles and into the air sacs or alveoli at the tips of the bronchioles

✔ The alveoli provide a large surface area over which the exchange of oxygen and carbon dioxide can occur.

✔ At the alveoli surface, oxygen diffuses from the inhaled air into the bloodstream and is carried around the body. Carbon dioxide diffuses in the opposite direction and is exhaled.

✔ In the blood, oxygen is carried by haemoglobin inside the red blood cells.

✔ Respiration is the process by which energy is released from the food we eat in all our body cells.

✔ The word equation for respiration is:

glucose + oxygen → carbon dioxide + water + energy

End-of-Chapter Questions

1 Explain in your own words the following key terms you have met in this chapter:

lungs

thorax

trachea

bronchi

bronchioles

alveoli

diffusion

gas exchange

haemoglobin

respiration

pressure

diaphragm

2 Stuart has had a climbing accident. He was unlucky enough to land on a sharp rock and this made a hole in his thorax (right through the skin and rib muscles). He has massive difficulty in breathing. No matter what he does, he can't seem to get air into his body.

a) Why is it vital to get air into our bodies?

b) Explain why Stuart cannot get air into his body. (*Hint*: Think about the pressure changes needed and how they're produced.)

c) Why do you think that Stuart's friend immediately put his thumb over the hole?

3 A Norwegian pen friend of yours consumes on average 8000 kJ per day and weighs 65 kg. She is lucky enough to be on a school exchange programme to Australia for a year. After 6 months she writes to you complaining that she's gained 5 kg in weight, but she's sure she's not eating more than usual. Write a letter back explaining why you think she may have gained weight.

4 The table opposite shows the number of breaths taken every minute by an athlete running on a treadmill at different speeds.

Speed (km/h)	Breaths/minute
6	20
9	28
12	35
15	40
20	42

a) Plot a line graph to present this information.

b) What pattern do you notice?

c) Explain these results. (*Hint*: you must talk about respiration and breathing in your answer.)

5 Look at the diagram showing the breathing system of a dolphin.

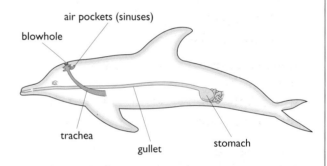

a) Why do you think that it's impossible for a dolphin to choke when eating?

b) How do you think that a dolphin can make whistling noises without bubbles coming from its blowhole?

c) Why do you think that a dolphin's breathing passageways are reinforced with cartilage?

d) What other differences do you think there might be between the breathing system of a dolphin and a human?

6 Explain the difference between gas exchange, breathing and respiration.

7 Find out how much energy different kinds of exercise use. Make a list, ranking the exercises from highest to lowest energy expenditure.

7 Health and drugs

Being healthy is all about having a body and mind that work well and are free from illness. If you look after it, your body should serve you well for the next 60 years or more. Looking after your body means eating a balanced diet, taking regular exercise and making sensible decisions about your lifestyle. Some people, however, find it difficult to accept that they have a responsibility towards their own **health** and make choices that mean their body no longer functions at its best.

Smoking

Ideas and Evidence

Figure 1 ▲ King James I of England

The crew that sailed with Christopher Columbus to the Americas in 1492 were probably the first Europeans to smoke tobacco. Bartholome de las Casas, a general in Columbus' crew, was the first person to notice tobacco's addictive effect. He wrote that the Spaniards who'd tried tobacco were developing a strong dependance on it and that it was hard to give up. Sailors brought the tobacco plant back to Spain with them and by 1559, its use was widespread. Tobacco quickly spread across Europe, arriving in England by 1565.

Surprisingly, the medical profession in Europe thought that tobacco had many curative effects and prescribed it regularly to people in a vain attempt to cure brain illnesses! Not everyone, however, was convinced of tobacco's curative powers, the most famous detractor being King James I of England. He wrote an article entitled *A counterblast to tobacco* which finishes with the following remark:

"a custom loathsome to the eye, hateful to the nose, harmful to the brain, dangerous to the lungs, and in the black stinking fume thereof nearest resembling the horrible stygian smoke of the pit that is bottomless."

James I (b.1566 d. 1625)

Some people have always suspected that smoking is bad for you, but the first scientific study which showed a link between lung cancer and smoking was conducted by the German physician F H Muller in 1939. During the 1930s and 1940s, around 60% of adult males in the UK were smokers, and by 1947 the rate of lung cancer deaths had become so high that the Medical Research Council decided to investigate. At the same time, the American government was also concerned about a rise in lung cancer and commissioned their own studies.

Ideas and Evidence

Figure 2 shows the results of three separate investigations. Doll and Hill studied a group of British doctors, Dorn studied a group of US army veterans and Hammond and Horn studied a group of male US volunteers (the total number of people studied was greater than one million). The y-axis shows the number of people per 100 000 that died from lung cancer each year while the x-axis shows the number of cigarettes smoked each day.

Figure 2 ▶ The relationship between smoking and lung cancer

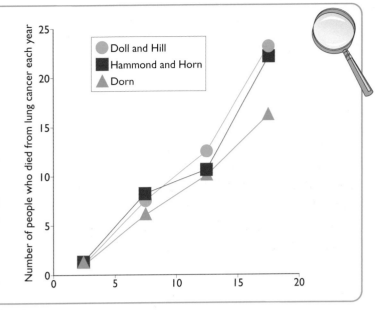

Test Yourself

1. How long have people in Europe been using tobacco?

2. What do *you* think that it was that James I found so distasteful about smoking?

3. Looking at Figure 2, what conclusions can you make about the relationship between smoking and lung cancer?

What is cancer?

Cancer is the uncontrolled development of cells, often leading to growths inside your body known as **tumours**. If untreated, this dreadful disease often ends in death. Figure 3 shows a tumour in the lungs of a cancer victim.

Cigarette smoke contains thousands of different chemicals, many of which can cause cancer. Cancer-causing substances are known as **carcinogens**. Most of these chemicals are found in a substance called tar which smokers inhale. It's the tar in cigarettes that also stains the fingers, hair and teeth of smokers.

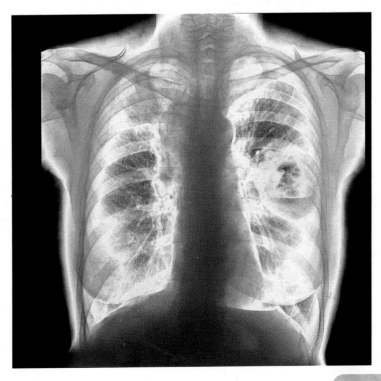

Figure 3 ▶ This tumour on the lungs was caused by smoking

Other smoking-related diseases

Emphysema

Not only does smoking cause cancer, it can also damage the alveoli in the lungs causing a disease known as **emphysema**. Emphysema makes the walls of your alveoli break down, making each alveolus many times bigger, reducing their surface area.

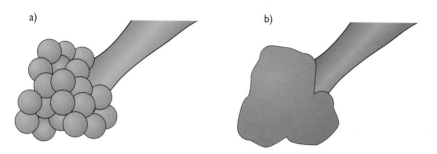

a)

b)

Figure 4 ◄ a) These alveoli are from a healthy non-smoker
b) This smoker's alveoli walls have broken down making one large alveolus instead of lots of small alveoli

Emphysema sufferers find it difficult to get enough oxygen into their bloodstream because the surface area of the alveoli has been dramatically reduced. These people often need to breathe in pure oxygen to make it through the day.

Heart disease

Cigarette smoke also contains a drug called **nicotine** which has a number of effects on the body. Nicotine makes your blood thicker and causes your blood vessels to constrict or get narrower. Both of these changes make it more difficult for your heart to pump blood around your body. The increased stickiness of the blood means that it's more likely to form clots which can block an artery or vein. If the clot appears in one of the arteries that supplies the heart muscle with blood (see Figure 5), then that part of the heart gets less oxygen and food than it needs to function properly. This can lead to a pain in the chest known as **angina**.

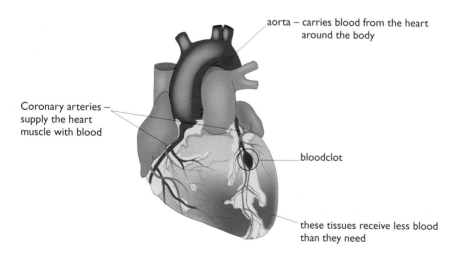

aorta – carries blood from the heart around the body

Coronary arteries – supply the heart muscle with blood

bloodclot

these tissues receive less blood than they need

Figure 5 ◄ The stickiness of the blood means clots are likely. Imagine trying to squeeze treacle down a small tube. It's no wonder that smokers have problems

If the coronary artery becomes completely blocked, then a section of the heart may actually die. This is known as a **heart attack**.

Peripheral vascular disease

It's not just in your heart that blood vessels become constricted after smoking. They do so throughout your body. Smoking can cause peripheral vascular disease which affects the limbs, especially the legs. In some smokers, the blood supply to their legs becomes almost completely blocked, so the tissues in their leg die, resulting in a condition called **gangrene**. Surgeons must then remove the limb by amputation.

Test Yourself

4   What are tumours?

5   What does the word 'carcinogen' mean?

6   Describe how smoking can reduce the internal surface area of the lungs.

7   How does smoking cause a) heart disease, b) gangrene?

Why do people persist in smoking?

Most people who take up smoking do so during puberty which can be a very confusing time. Some people think that it will make them look cool or more mature, imagining that they can always give up before it becomes a problem. Smoking is, however, very addictive indeed – some studies claim that it is even more addictive than cocaine. Once you're hooked, it's very difficult to quit.

Strangely enough, the tobacco companies themselves don't see all smokers as 'cool'. The following is an extract from a report made by a market research company describing some of their customers:

"Cluster I – 'Slobs'

27% of cigarette smokers aged 18–24 years are represented by this cluster. Describing members of this cluster as 'Slobs' may seem unkind, but this title is earned by their low concern with their appearance and the little effort they make to keep themselves informed."

"Slobs ... downmarket ... less likely to have gone to further education ... committed smokers ... show commitment or concern about little else e.g. health, diet, appearance, promotions."

8   What do you think about this company's attitude towards its customers? Discuss this in small groups, then compare your opinions with the rest of the class.

Drugs

A **drug** is a substance that changes the way your body works. Many drugs in our society are legal because their effects are quite small and predictable. We take certain drugs to improve our health. A doctor might give you prescription drugs to fight bacteria (germs) that have got into your body, or you might take a mild painkiller such as aspirin to dull the pain of a headache. We take recreational drugs because we enjoy their effect. Coffee, tea and cola contain a drug called **caffeine**. Caffeine tends to make people feel more alert and stops them feeling tired. We classify drugs that perk you up as **stimulants**.

Figure 6 ◄ Caffeine is a stimulant

Alcohol

Alcohol is a legal drug that has quite a different effect – it slows down the way your mind and body work, making you sluggish and tired. Drugs that slow you down are known as **depressants**.

Figure 7 ◄ Alcohol is a depressant

Alcohol – the bad news first

In large doses, alcohol can have many effects upon the body including the removal of inhibitions, increasing aggression, loss of balance and poor co-ordination. Many people also suffer from very bad headaches the morning after drinking too much – this is known as a hangover. Drinking alcohol in moderation is socially acceptable in Britain and seems not to be a problem for most people. However, alcohol is addictive and people who drink too much on a regular basis can become dependant on this drug. These people are known as alcoholics. Becoming dependant upon any drug can ruin people's lives, and dependancy upon alcohol can be as serious as addiction to many illegal drugs.

Quite apart from the destruction of their social lives, alcoholics may also be damaging their bodies. Like all foods, after being absorbed into the bloodstream alcohol is taken to the liver. The liver de-toxifies alcohol so that it limits the amount of damage it can do to your body. However, if too much alcohol is consumed, this important organ becomes damaged, resulting in a condition known as **cirrhosis**. This is when healthy liver cells become replaced by useless scar tissue so that the liver eventually ceases to function properly.

Drinking too much alcohol can also affect other organs:

- the muscles of the heart can become weakened leading to heart disease;
- your brain cells can eventually be killed which leads to mental deterioration;
- your pancreas can become damaged and inflamed (pancreatitis). This is dangerous because without your pancreas, it's impossible to digest your food properly.

And now for the good news

Medical researchers have found that drinking in moderation may be beneficial. People who drink a little alcohol each week actually have a lower risk of heart problems than non-drinkers. Alcohol is measured in units. Men should not drink more than 21 units of alcohol per week, and women should not drink more than 14 units. A unit of alcohol is equivalent to half a pint of beer or lager, one small glass of wine, a glass of sherry or a shot of whisky or vodka.

a)

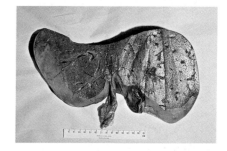

b)

Figure 8 ▲ Liver a) is from a healthy individual. Liver b) is from a person with cirrhosis

1/2 pint of beer   small glass of wine   small glass of sherry   one measure of whisky

Figure 9 ◄ All these drinks contain one unit of alchohol

Test Yourself

9 Explain what is meant by the word 'drug'.

10 What is the difference between stimulants and depressants?

11 List the short-term effects of drinking alcohol.

12 Explain how excessive drinking can damage your health.

13 Briony drank 7 units of alcohol one evening. What combination of drinks could she have consumed if she had drunk three different types of alcohol?

14 If Briony continued to drink this amount every night of the week, how do you think this would affect her life?

Illegal drugs

Ideas and Evidence   The opium poppy

The use of drugs that are now illegal is not a recent phenomenon. The ancient Sumerians are known to have used the opium poppy (from which the drug 'heroin' can be extracted) more than 5000 years ago. They called it the 'plant of joy'. The Chinese used opium for centuries, both eating and smoking it. The Ancient Greeks and Romans used opium as a sedative and sleeping drug. In the 18th and 19th Centuries, the British government traded in opium and even waged war on other nations that tried to sell the drug, to protect its own market!

During the 18th Century, opium was freely available from your local chemist, and people took it to gain relief from many ailments such as toothache or sleeplessness. 'Godfrey's Cordial' sounds harmless enough and was given as a soothing syrup to quieten restless babies – even this contained opium. In fact many children were killed by overdosing on such medicines.

Little was known about the dangerous side effects of opium at this time and many famous writers and poets took opium to experience 'hallucinations' and then write about them. Samuel Taylor Coleridge took some opium before writing his famous poem, *Kubla Khan*.

Coleridge eventually became quite ill from his use of opium, and later in his life condemned the fact that it was so easily available. Coleridge called upon the government to make casual use of this drug illegal.

Figure 10 ▶ Samuel Taylor Coleridge

Test Yourself

15 Who were the first people known to have taken opium?

16 What is the name of the drug that can be extracted from the opium poppy?

17 What do you think are the effects of taking opium?

18 Do you think that it was a good idea to make the casual use of opium illegal?

Cannabis

Many of the illegal drugs that people take today are produced by plants. Cannabis is a product of the plant called hemp. Figure 11 shows what cannabis looks like.

Cannabis is a drug which is normally smoked, but can also be eaten. Some people feel nothing at all after taking cannabis, but others feel some of the following effects:

- feelings of euphoria – drug users call these feelings 'a high'
- hunger – drug users call this effect 'the munchies'
- a deep feeling of relaxation and sleepiness
- uncontrollable giggling
- paranoia.

The health risks associated with cannabis include:

- an increase in the risks of getting lung cancer
- damage to the immune system (the system that protects your body from disease)
- a developing dependence on the drug.

Other names for cannabis include: marijuana, weed, pot, grass, reefer, ganja, mary jane, blunt, joint, roach, nail, hashish and kif.

Figure 11 ▲ Cannabis is produced from the hemp plant

Ecstasy

Ecstasy is a synthetic drug, made by chemists in the laboratory. It is taken in tablet form and is a drug much associated with 'club culture' and dancing. After taking ecstasy, people feel the following effects:

- increased emotional closeness to people around them
- a sense of happiness and well-being
- increased response to music
- mild hallucinations
- a feeling of energy.

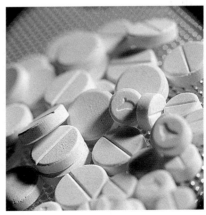

Figure 12 ▲ Ecstasy tablets

The health risks associated with ecstasy include:

- an increase in heart rate and blood pressure
- increased perspiration – which can lead to heat stroke and dehydration
- liver damage
- inability to sleep
- brain damage.

Some people have died after taking just one ecstasy tablet.

Other names for ecstasy include: E, mdma, dennis the menace, rhubarb and custard, new yorkers, love doves, disco burgers, phase 4, diamonds, fantasy, echoes, essence, adam, eve, xtc.

Cocaine

Figure 13 ◄ Coca plants

Cocaine is made from the leaves of the coca plant which grows in South America. The native people of Peru have chewed coca leaves for centuries. They get a very small dose of the drug from doing this. It gives them a feeling of energy and they often take it with them if they're planning a long hike over difficult terrain. When the drug is purified, it forms a white powder which can be taken by inhalation through the nose (snorting), smoking or by injection.

The effects of taking cocaine include:

- extreme euphoria
- a feeling of energy
- a feeling of confidence
- heightened alertness.

The health risks associated with cocaine include:

- damage to the heart, leading to heart attack
- lung failure
- strokes, seizure and headaches
- stomach pains and nausea
- a rapidly developing dependence upon the drug
- erosion of the septum of your nose.

Solvents

A **solvent** is something that can dissolve something else. Water is a solvent and is obviously harmless, but there are many others which release vapours that can have some dangerous effects if inhaled.

Figure 14 ▲ Sniffing solvents can be extremely dangerous

A whole range of substances are used, such as: solvent-based glues, dry cleaning fluids, thinners, paint, correcting fluids (Tipp-Ex, etc.), aerosol sprays (deodorants, hair sprays, furniture polish, etc.), butane gas (particularly in cigarette lighter refill canisters) and petrol.

The inhaled vapour is absorbed into the bloodstream in the lungs and quickly reaches the brain. The effects of solvent inhalation include:

- a feeling similar to being drunk
- heart and breathing rate slow down
- mild hallucinations.

The dangers associated with solvent abuse are:

- becoming unconscious
- choking on your own vomit which can lead to death
- death from suffocation – especially if plastic bags are used
- heart failure
- damage to liver and kidneys
- freezing of the bronchi, if solvents are squirted directly into the mouth, leading to death through suffocation.

Test Yourself

19 Which of the drugs mentioned above do you think are stimulants and which are depressants?

20 Make a table in your book to summarise the drugs mentioned in this chapter and their effects.

21 Which of the drugs mentioned in the text do you think are most dangerous to health? Explain your answer.

Summary

When you have finished studying this chapter, you should understand that:

✓ To be healthy you have to eat a balanced diet, take regular exercise and make sensible choices about your lifestyle.

✓ Smoking can cause a number of diseases, including cancer, emphysema, heart disease and peripheral vascular disease.

✓ Drugs are substances that alter the way the body works.

✓ There are different types of drug including prescription drugs like aspirin and antibiotics, recreational drugs like caffeine and alcohol, and illegal drugs like cannabis, ecstasy and cocaine.

✓ Some drugs perk you up and make you feel more awake. These are called stimulants.

✓ Other drugs slow you down and make you tired. These are depressants.

✓ Drinking large quantities of alcohol can cause a serious liver disease called cirrhosis.

✓ Illegal drugs such as cannabis, ecstasy and cocaine cause serious health problems and can be very addictive.

✓ Solvent inhalation is extremely dangerous and often results in death.

End-of-Chapter Questions

1 Explain in your own words the following key terms you have met in this chapter:

health

cancer

tumours

carcinogens

emphysema

nicotine

angina

heart attack

gangrene

drug

caffeine

stimulant

depressant

cirrhosis

solvent

2 A unit of alcohol increases the concentration of alcohol in your blood by 16 mg per 100 cm³. Steve has been to the pub to celebrate his birthday. Below is a table that shows the concentration of alcohol in his blood after he left the pub.

Time	Blood alcohol concentration (mg/cm³)
12.00 am	112
1.00 am	96
2.00 am	80
3.00 am	64
4.00 am	48
5.00 am	32
6.00 am	16
7.00 am	0

a) Plot a graph to present the above data.

b) Steve drank beer all night. How many pints did he consume?

c) How many units of alcohol does Steve get rid of from his body every hour?

3 Write a newspaper style article about the effects of smoking on health.

4 How do you think that smoking affects athletic performance?

5 A woman smokes 20 cigarettes each day. If a packet of cigarettes costs £4.50, calculate how much this costs her each year.

6 What advice would you give a friend who was keen to try a) cannabis, b) cocaine and c) ecstasy?

7 Despite having potentially dangerous side effects, alcohol and smoking are legal in Britain. Why do you think this is the case?

8 The graph below shows the relationship between smokers and their income (Source: Department of Health survey for England, 1998).

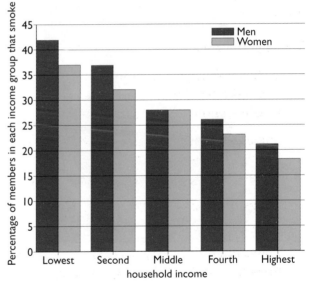

a) What is the relationship shown between income and smoking?

b) Attempt to explain this relationship.

c) What can you say about the health of poorer people in society?

9 a) Find out how much money the Government gains per year from taxing cigarettes.

b) If you were in charge of the Government, how would you spend this money?

8

Microbes and disease

Microbes are living things that are too small to be seen by the naked eye. They can be classified into one of three categories: **bacteria**, **viruses** and **fungi**. Most microbes are completely harmless, and some can even be helpful to us, but a small fraction are responsible for illnesses. These are the germs your parents refer to when they tell you to wash your hands before eating. In this chapter we will find out more about how microbes can help us and harm us.

Ideas and Evidence

Who discovered microbes?

Figure 1 ▲ Anton van Leeuwenhoek

A Dutch textile worker, Anton van Leeuwenhoek (1632–1723), is the first person known to have seen bacteria. He used magnifying lenses as part of his everyday work in order to judge the quality of the textiles he worked with. In secret at first, he started making his own lenses and built his own microscopes, which were powerful enough to magnify objects to 300 times their original size.

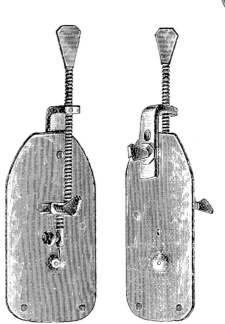

Figure 2 ▲ Van Leeuwenhoek's microscope

Van Leeuwenhoek thought that the spicy flavour of pepper might be caused by tiny spikes. To investigate this, he prepared some peppercorns by letting them soften in water for 3 months. After this time, he mounted them on a pinhead and was amazed by what he saw.

This is an excerpt from his journal:

"the creatures which drifted around were incredibly small, nay so small, in my sight, that I judged that even if 100 of these very wee animals lay stretched out one against another, they could not reach to the length of a grain of coarse sand; and if this be true, then ten thousand of these living creatures could scarce equal the bulk of a coarse sand-grain..."

After this, he found bacteria on scrapings from his teeth which he called "animalcules". Van Leeuwenhoek died after catching a disease from studying bacteria from sheep blood which caused uncontrollable spasms of his diaphragm. This disease is now known as Van Leeuwenhoek's disease.

It wasn't until much later that the connection between bacteria and illness was made. Robert Koch (1843–1910), a German physician, demonstrated that the infectious disease anthrax was passed to mice only if a certain type of bacteria were present in their bloodstream. He went on to demonstrate that tuberculosis (a disease of the lungs) and cholera (a disease that causes chronic diarrhoea) were caused by certain types of bacteria.

Bacteria

Bacteria are single-celled organisms that are less than 0.001 mm in length. If you look at Figure 3 you'll see that, unlike animal cells, bacteria have a cell wall made of protein and sugar. Another difference is that they have no nucleus. Their genetic material simply floats in the cytoplasm.

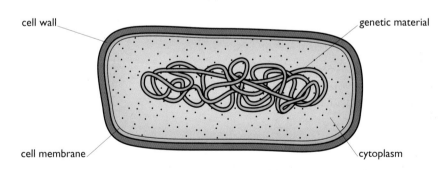

cell wall

genetic material

cell membrane

cytoplasm

Figure 3 ◄ The structure of a simple bacterial cell

Bacteria get their food by releasing digestive enzymes onto organic matter (this may be food, waste from living things or dead things) so that it breaks it down into simpler materials. These are then absorbed into the cytoplasm and the bacteria use them to grow and reproduce. Bacteria reproduce simply by dividing into two new cells when they get big enough. As they grow and reproduce, they produce waste products, some of which are poisonous. These waste products are known as **toxins** and it is these that make you ill.

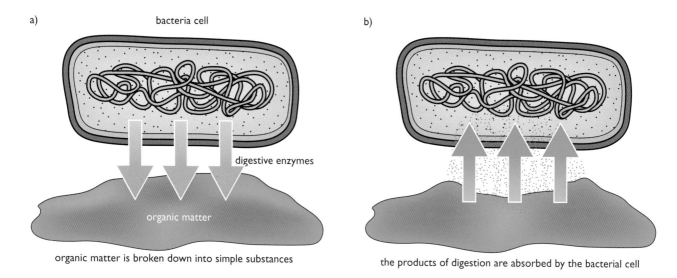

a) bacteria cell
b)

digestive enzymes

organic matter

organic matter is broken down into simple substances

the products of digestion are absorbed by the bacterial cell

Figure 4 ▲ The bacterium digests the organic matter externally

Test Yourself

1 Name three diseases caused by bacteria.

2 Describe how bacteria get their food.

3 Explain why certain types of bacteria can make you ill.

4 List the differences between an animal cell and a bacterial cell.

Hygiene – please wash your hands!

Bacteria that cause food poisoning, such as *Salmonella*, are always present in the faeces of people with infections. These bacteria can easily end up on the hands of the sufferer if he or she forgets to wash their hands after visiting the lavatory. People who handle food must be especially careful to keep their hands clean as they could infect thousands of people by transferring the bacteria onto the food that others consume. Most bacteria are easily killed by soap, detergents (washing-up liquid), antiseptics, disinfectants and high temperatures.

It's very important that we try to keep everything that we take into our body as clean as possible so as to reduce the risk of infection. This includes the plates that we eat from, and the utensils and machines that we use to prepare food. In 1996 there was an outbreak of food poisoning in Scotland caused by a bacterium known as *E. coli* 0157. More than 20 people died and hundreds of people became ill during the outbreak. The source of the infection was traced to a dirty packaging machine in one butcher's shop.

Viruses

Viruses are very simple micro-organisms, much smaller than a bacterial cell. They are made of genetic material surrounded by a protein coat.

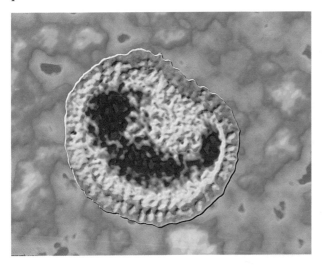

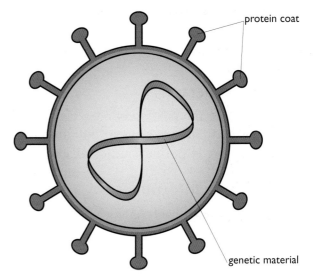

protein coat

genetic material

Figure 5 ▲ The virus that causes influenza

Viruses cannot reproduce outside the body. They reproduce by latching onto one of your body's cells and injecting their genetic material into it. This turns your body's cells into factories which make thousands of copies of the virus. After a while, your cell bursts, releasing the viruses that it has made. These go on to infect more body cells. As your cells burst, toxins may be released which make you feel ill. Viruses cause diseases such as influenza (the 'flu), AIDS, measles, mumps, cold sores, smallpox, yellow fever, rabies, poliomyelitis, and the common cold.

Figure 6 ▼ A virus infects a host cell and reproduces inside it

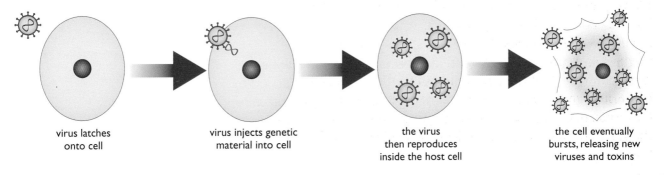

virus latches onto cell

virus injects genetic material into cell

the virus then reproduces inside the host cell

the cell eventually bursts, releasing new viruses and toxins

Test Yourself

8 List the differences between viruses and bacteria.

9 Name three illnesses caused by viruses.

10 Make a flowchart to show how viruses reproduce. Start with the following statement:

A virus latches ⎯⎯⎯⎯⎯→
on to a cell

Spreading disease

There are a number of different ways in which diseases can be spread. These are listed below, along with an example of a disease spread in this way.

1 Person-to-person

This may involve the passing of bacteria or viruses through blood, saliva or through fluids during sexual intercourse. The common cold is often spread in this way, for example through kissing.

2 Food-borne infection

Food poisoning from bacteria such as *E. Coli* and *Salmonella* is the best example of this. If food is properly treated and cooked thoroughly before eating, the chances of food poisoning can be reduced.

3 Water-borne infection

Contaminated water can spread diseases like typhoid, cholera, dysentery and polio. Such diseases are particularly rife in developing countries.

4 Airborne infection

This involves the passing of bacteria or viruses through the air. The common cold can be spread this way by coughing and sneezing. The measles and chickenpox viruses are also spread from person to person through the air.

5 Insect-borne infection

A number of diseases are spread by insects. The plague, which killed many people in England in the 17th Century, was carried by rat fleas. Malaria is another very common example of an insect-borne disease.

Female mosquitoes inject *plasmodium* (which causes malaria) into humans when they bite them. Malaria is very common in developing countries in South America, Asia and Africa.

Body defences

Your body defends itself from microbes in a number of ways:

- The skin acts as a barrier to infection, and repairs itself quickly if it gets broken by first producing a scab and then making new skin cells.
- Your breathing passageways are lined with mucus-producing cells and ciliated cells. The mucus traps dust or dirt that may have been breathed in, the ciliated cells then sweep the dirt which might contain microbes upwards away from your lungs.

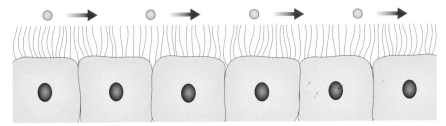

Figure 7 ◄ The cilia beat and waft the dirt upwards, away from the lungs

- Your stomach contains hydrochloric acid which can kill bacteria in food.

If a microbe is lucky enough to get past these first lines of defence, your body's **white blood cells** spring into action. Some white blood cells (called phagocytes) travel around your bloodstream seeking out microbes and eating them! They engulf the invader and then break them down using enzymes.

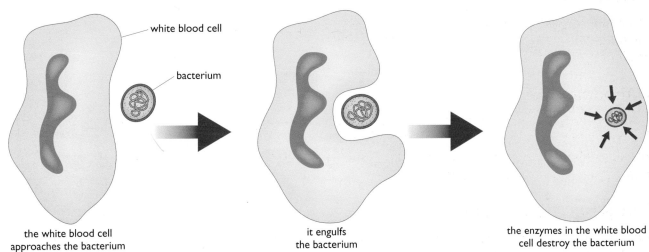

white blood cell

bacterium

the white blood cell approaches the bacterium

it engulfs the bacterium

the enzymes in the white blood cell destroy the bacterium

Figure 8 ▲ The white blood cell engulfs the bacterium and destroys it

Other white blood cells (called lymphocytes) make chemicals called **antibodies**. Antibodies surround bacteria and viruses, neutralising them and making it easy for other white blood cells to eat them.

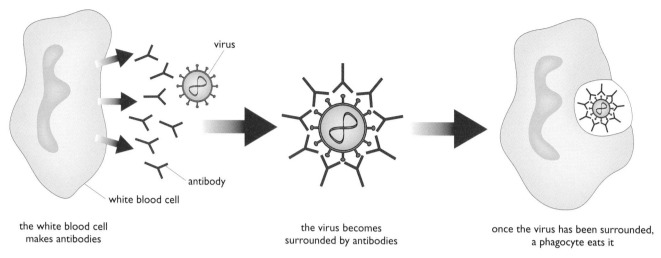

the white blood cell
makes antibodies

the virus becomes
surrounded by antibodies

once the virus has been surrounded,
a phagocyte eats it

Figure 9 ▲   Antibodies help you fight off infection by neutralising microbes like viruses, making it easier for other white blood cells to destroy them

Immunity

Once your body has been infected by a particular microbe, certain white blood cells 'remember' which antibody was best able to fight it. This means that if you come in contact with the same microbe again, your white blood cells can make antibodies much more quickly and destroy all the microbes before they make you ill. This is known as 'becoming immune', and can happen with diseases such as measles, chickenpox and mumps.

Ideas and Evidence   Vaccination

In the 18th Century, it was common for people to contract a dangerous, often fatal, disease called **smallpox**. The first symptoms of the disease were a fever, backache and a reddish purple rash on the chest and back. After this, the rash disappeared and the fever dropped, only to return about three days later along with a new bumpy rash which started on the feet and hands but rapidly spread to the rest of the body. The bumps formed blisters which filled with pus and would eventually drop off forming a scab. The scab would heal but it would leave a permanent scar.

Figure 10 ▲   This child is suffering from smallpox

Ideas and Evidence   Vaccination continued

Smallpox was spread by a very infectious virus. Most forms of this virus would not prove fatal but bacteria frequently got into the scabs and caused a subsequent infection from which the sufferer often died. There was, however, a very serious form of the disease known as 'sledgehammer smallpox' which resulted in massive, uncontrollable bleeding from the blisters, as well as from the mouth and nose. This would rapidly lead to death.

At this time, people knew you could only catch smallpox once and used to seek out people who had mild forms of the disease to infect themselves intentionally and become immune to it. Naturally, this was a high risk strategy and whilst many people survived the disease, some did not.

A Gloucestershire doctor called Edward Jenner observed that milkmaids never caught smallpox, but noticed that they often caught a mild illness called cowpox (*vaccinae*) from the cows that they milked. He wondered if catching cowpox could give immunity to smallpox. He decided to try his idea out but needed somebody who hadn't previously been infected by smallpox or cowpox. A nine year old boy, James Phipps, fitted the bill perfectly. Dr Jenner knew a milkmaid called Sarah Nelmes who had cowpox at the time and used a scalpel to scratch the pus from one of her blisters. He then scratched James' arm with the same scalpel. Sure enough, James went on to catch cowpox and fully recovered from the infection after a couple of weeks. Dr Jenner then tried to infect James with smallpox. To everyone's relief, James proved to be immune to this serious disease and went on to live a long and happy life.

This method became known as **vaccination** (*vacca* means cow in Latin), and worked because the smallpox virus and the cowpox virus have a very similar structure. This means that the antibodies that destroyed the cowpox virus would also work very effectively against the smallpox virus. Vaccination has become an important tool in the fight against disease. Smallpox has since been **eradicated** by a worldwide vaccination programme. The last known case of smallpox happened in 1977.

Figure 11 ▶   The story of vaccination

Useful microbes

Antibiotics

In the early part of the 20th Century, bacterial infections were fought by medicines known as 'sulpha drugs'. They worked by stopping bacteria absorbing certain vitamins – bacteria need a balanced diet too! This killed the bacteria, but it also harmed the health of those who took them as it stopped the patient absorbing vitamins as well

Ideas and Evidence

Alexander Fleming was born in 1881 and trained to become a doctor at St Mary's Hospital in London. He remained there all his working life, developing a keen interest in bacteria. Fleming grew lots of different types of bacteria on special agar plates. He even made bacterial 'paintings', by smearing pigmented bacteria in certain shapes and letting them grow.

By all accounts, Fleming was a little disorganised in his approach and used to leave bacterial colonies growing well beyond the point at which other researchers would have discarded them. Returning to work after taking a holiday, he noticed that one of his plates had become contaminated with a fungus called *Penicillium*.

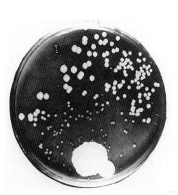

Figure 12 ▲   Alexander Fleming's agar plate which became contaminated with penicillin

Fleming noticed that the bacteria around the fungus had been killed and he thought that the fungus must be making something that was responsible for this. With the help of an American drug company, the substance that the fungus made was purified and called penicillin.

How does it work?

Penicillin works by stopping bacteria making their cell walls properly. Because our cells don't have cell walls, it doesn't present us with the same problem! Since Fleming's discovery, lots of other similar substances have been discovered. The name given to this group of drugs is **antibiotics**.

Different antibiotics kill different types of bacteria. Doctors can find out which particular antibiotic to use by growing bacteria with discs of paper coated with different antibiotics as shown in Figure 13. The antibiotic that works best will have the largest clear area around it where no bacteria have been able to grow.

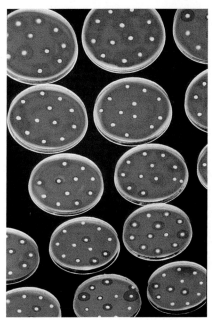

Figure 13 ▲   It's clear which antibiotic works best with this bacteria

Test Yourself

15 Before antibiotics, people were reluctant to take the sulpha drugs that their doctor prescribed. Explain why.

16 Imagine that you are Fleming. Describe what you see upon return from your holiday and say what it makes you think.

17 Why do you think that the *penicillium* fungus makes substances that kill bacteria?

18 Coralie has been taken ill by a bacterial infection. You are the doctor that has to choose the correct antibiotic for her treatment. What will you do?

19 How do antibiotics work?

Yeast

Penicillium is not the only fungus that is useful to us. Another type of fungus that we make use of all the time is **yeast**. Yeast is a very simple organism that reproduces by growing and dividing its body into two. This is an example of asexual reproduction (see Chapter 5). As it grows, the yeast respires, producing the two waste products – carbon dioxide and ethanol (alcohol). We can make use of both of these products in different ways. We add yeast to the dough when making bread and the carbon dioxide produced helps the bread to rise. When we brew beers, wines and spirits, we add the yeast to the fermenting mixture. This produces alcohol.

Test Yourself

20 What two chemicals does yeast produce as it respires?

21 In what ways do we use these two products?

Summary

When you have finished studying this chapter, you should understand that:

- Microbes are living things that can only be seen with a microscope.

- There are three categories of microbes: bacteria, viruses and fungi.

- Some microbes are useful to us while others can cause disease.

- Bacteria are tiny, single-celled organisms. As they grow and reproduce, they produce toxins which can make us ill.

- Examples of diseases caused by bacteria are tuberculosis and cholera.

- We can reduce the chance of becoming ill by making sure we keep our hands clean and cook our food thoroughly.

- Viruses are very simple organisms which reproduce inside the cells of a host organism.

- Diseases caused by viruses include AIDS, measles, mumps and cold sores.

- Diseases can be spread in five ways: person-to-person, food-borne, water-borne, airborne and insect-borne.

- Our bodies have a number of defences against microbes including skin, hydrochloric acid in the stomach and white blood cells.

- Once you have had a particular disease, you develop an immunity to it.

- Antibiotics can be used to treat bacterial infections.

- Yeast is a helpful microbe used in baking and brewing.

End-of-Chapter Questions

1 Explain in your own words the following key terms you have met in this chapter:

microbes

bacteria

virus

fungus

toxin

antibodies

smallpox

vaccination

eradication

antibiotic

yeast

2 Imagine that you are a doctor. One of your patients has measles and asks you to prescribe antibiotics to get rid of the infection. Explain to him why antibiotics will not work.

3 A restaurant has just served you with some chicken that is not fully cooked (you can tell because it's still a little bit pink in the middle). Explain to the waiter why fully cooking the food makes it safer to eat.

4 A friend of yours sitting next to you in a biology lesson is suffering from a bad cold. She sneezes as you breathe in.

a) Describe what happens to the cells in your breathing passageways next.

b) What does your body do to prevent you becoming ill?

End-of-Chapter Questions continued

Months old	Died	Years old	Died	Years old	Died	Years old	Died	Years old	Died
0	202	0	2 235	10	226	40	43	75	4
1	181	1	1 524	15	226	45	22	80	10
2	162	2	1 197	20	240	50	13	85	1
3	456	3	869	25	148	55	10	90	0
6	646	4	628	30	98	60	19	95	1
9	588	5	1 122	35	75	70	10	Unknown	8

5 The table above, from the *Encyclopaedia Metropolitan*, shows the number of people dying from smallpox in London in 1844.

a) Construct a line graph showing how the number of people dying from this disease varies with age. Do this for people between the ages of 1–30.

b) Which age group is most vulnerable to this disease?

c) Imagine that you are a doctor at that time. How would you persuade mothers to let you vaccinate their children?

6 Find out how the livestock disease 'Foot and Mouth' is spread. Why do you think that the British Government decided not to vaccinate against the disease during the outbreak in 2001?

7 Howard Florey and Ernst Chain were also involved in the development of penicillin. Carry out some research to find out the contributions they made to the story.

9

Photosynthesis

Look at the pictures of the plants below. The plant on the right is a healthy plant, which has been kept in the light. The plant on the left looks very unhealthy; it's been kept in the dark for a week.

Venus fly-traps are clever plants. They lure unsuspecting insects into their traps and then snap shut, digesting anything that gets caught in their formidable jaws. Venus fly-traps are very unusual plants. Two thousand years ago, a Greek philosopher called Aristotle noticed that, unlike venus fly-traps, most plants never eat anything. He thought that they took in all their food from the soil through their roots. But do they?

It seems obvious that plants need light to stay healthy. They even bend towards the light if they are sitting on a windowsill. But what has this got to do with food?

What is photosynthesis?

Plants use light to make food in a process called **photosynthesis**. Photosynthesis means making (*synthesis*) food using light (*photo*). The type of food which plants make is sugar (glucose). Plants can use the sugar for energy in **respiration**. Respiration is the process in which living things break down food to release energy.

You can show that plants contain sugar by testing an onion for sugar. If you grind up some onion with water, and then test the water with Benedict's solution, it turns orange. A colour change from blue to orange shows that lots of sugar is present.

Most plants do not use all their sugar straight away. They often stick sugar molecules together to make starch, which they store in their leaves, stem or roots. To test a leaf for starch, you need to kill it with boiling water, boil it in ethanol and then add iodine. If starch is present, the leaf will turn blue/black.

Scientists usually monitor whether photosynthesis is happening by testing leaves for starch. But what does a plant need to make starch?

Figure 1 ▲ This leaf has tested positive for starch

Test Yourself

1   What are you testing for if you use a) Benedict's solution and b) iodine solution?

2   What does a plant often do with sugar after making it in photosynthesis?

What does a plant need for photosynthesis to happen?

Is chlorophyll needed for photosynthesis?

Green plants all contain **chlorophyll**. Animals do not contain chlorophyll and don't photosynthesise. This suggests that chlorophyll may be needed for photosynthesis to happen. But how can we test this?

The best way is to see if a leaf without chlorophyll can still make starch. If we took chlorophyll out of a leaf ourselves, the leaf would die. Luckily, there are some leaves in nature that do not contain much chlorophyll. These are called variegated leaves.

Figure 2 shows what happened after testing a variegated leaf for starch. Starch was only found in the part that contained chlorophyll. This suggests that chlorophyll is needed to make starch.

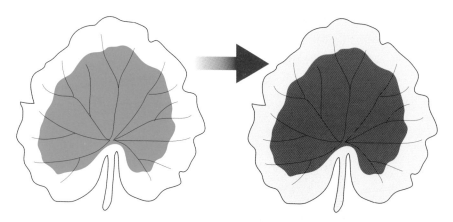

Figure 2 ◄ Only the green part of the geranium leaf tested positive for starch

Is carbon dioxide needed for photosynthesis?

When you breathe out, carbon dioxide leaves your body. But what would happen if carbon dioxide just kept building up in the air around you? Eventually it would poison you. Is it possible that plants use the carbon dioxide to help make starch?

Look at the plants in Figure 3. The one on the left is inside a bell jar. The small pot of sodium hydroxide stops the plant getting carbon dioxide by taking it out of the air. The plant on the right is in normal air and can easily get hold of carbon dioxide. After leaving the plants for three days, a leaf was removed from each and tested for starch. Only the leaf from the plant that had access to carbon dioxide tested positive for starch. Without carbon dioxide, the plant in the bell jar could not make starch. The plant in normal air could make starch. The only difference between the two plants was whether they had access to carbon dioxide. Because the plant with carbon dioxide could make starch, we know that carbon dioxide is needed for photosynthesis.

Figure 3 ◄ Testing to see whether plants need carbon dioxide to photosynthesise

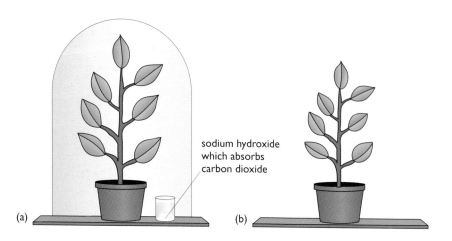

sodium hydroxide which absorbs carbon dioxide

(a)　　(b)

Is light needed for photosynthesis?

We still haven't shown that light really is needed to make starch. Look at the leaf in Figure 4. By fixing black card over part of the leaf, we can stop light getting to that part of it. This leaf was left with card on for three days and then the card was removed. The leaf was then pulled off the plant and tested for starch. Because only those parts with access to light could make starch, light must be needed for photosynthesis.

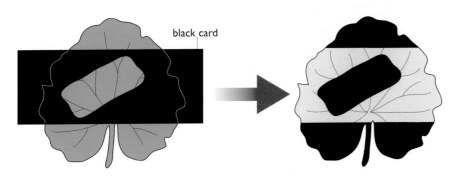

black card

Figure 4 ◄ Testing to see whether plants need light for photosynthesis

Is water needed for photosynthesis?

Look at the pictures of plants in Figure 5. The plant on the left has been well watered, while the one on the right has been forgotten about. The watered one looks much healthier. However, it is almost impossible to test whether water is used in photosynthesis. Imagine if you took all the water out of a leaf – you would kill it straight away. This is because water has several different uses in a plant – it holds the plant upright and transports food around the plant. If we removed all the water from you, you would not survive for very long either!

Figure 5 ▼

Test Yourself

3   Make a list of those substances used by the leaf during photosynthesis.

4   What is the job of sodium hydroxide when testing whether carbon dioxide is needed for photosynthesis?

5   Explain how, when tested for starch, you could make your name appear on a leaf in a light colour against a dark background.

6   Explain why it is impossible for you to show that water is needed for photosynthesis in a school laboratory.

What else is made during photosynthesis?

We know that plants make sugar which they turn into starch, but do they make anything else during photosynthesis? In 1771, Joseph Priestly carried out some experiments that suggested they produce oxygen. You can read about his experiments later in the chapter.

But how can *we* test if plants produce oxygen? Look at the apparatus in Figure 6. By putting the test tube above the pondweed, any bubbles of gas given off can be collected. Eventually, after collecting a whole test tube of gas we can test it for oxygen by inserting a glowing splint. When you do this, it re-lights, proving that the plant produces oxygen during photosynthesis.

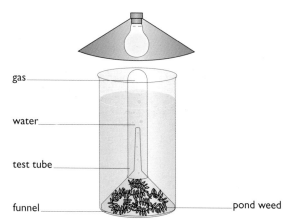

gas

water

test tube

funnel

pond weed

Figure 6 ◄   You can use this apparatus to see whether plants give off oxygen

Photosynthesis: the word equation

Now we know what is used in photosynthesis (the reactants) and what is produced in photosynthesis (the products), we can write an equation:

$$\text{carbon dioxide} + \text{water} \xrightarrow[\text{chlorophyll}]{\text{light}} \text{starch} + \text{oxygen}$$

The light and chlorophyll go above and below the arrow because they do not change in the reaction. The chlorophyll just grabs the carbon dioxide and water, catches the light energy and makes the reaction happen.

But remember, photosynthesis does not make starch immediately. It makes glucose (a type of sugar), which it can store as starch.

$$\text{carbon dioxide} + \text{water} \xrightarrow[\text{chlorophyll}]{\text{light}} \text{glucose} + \text{oxygen}$$

Extension box

You can also write a symbol equation for this reaction:

$$6CO_2 + 6H_2O \xrightarrow[\text{chlorophyll}]{\text{light}} C_6H_{12}O_6 + 6O_2$$

Commercial fruit and vegetable growers use this information to help them produce good crops. Imagine you are a gardener growing tomatoes in a greenhouse. You want your plants to get as big as possible. To do this, the plants need to make as much glucose as possible. To help them, you make sure they get lots of water and light. But is that enough? Think about a cook making chocolate cakes all day. If you make sure he gets lots of eggs and chocolate, he still can't make more cakes unless he gets more flour as well. Likewise, gardeners have to give their tomatoes extra carbon dioxide too. They buy the carbon dioxide in gas cylinders and pump it into their greenhouses.

Ideas and Evidence

The experiments and the equations above make photosynthesis seem very simple, but imagine you were a scientist several hundred years ago, and you had to work out all this from scratch. Here's how it was done...

★ In 1692, a Dutchman called van Helmont thought about Aristotle's original ideas. He did not believe that plants took in food through their roots, and invented an experiment to prove it. He planted a willow tree seedling and left it to grow for five years. Before planting, he weighed the plant and weighed the soil he planted it in. After five years, he weighed them both again. He discovered that the soil had lost 56 g, but the plant had gained **74 kg**! He concluded that even if the plant gets a small amount of food from the soil, most of its food comes from somewhere else.

★ About 80 years later, Joseph Priestly did some more work on photosynthesis. In 1771, he realised that the air in a gas jar can be changed by burning a candle inside it. This gas jar could not keep a mouse alive or keep a candle flame burning. However, he realised that if you add a sprig of mint, the air is gradually restored. He concluded that plants give off oxygen which helped keep the mouse alive and the candle flame burning.

1 Candle was allowed to burn out

2 A sprig of mint was inserted into the bell jar. The apparatus was left for ten days

3 The candle can now be relighted

★ Surprisingly, Priestly did not realise how important light was in this process. It took a Dutch doctor called Jan Ingenhousz to demonstrate that only the green parts of plants produce chlorophyll and that they absorb light energy.

Find out:

1 Would the candle in Priestly's experiment have re-lit again if the jar had been kept in the dark for 10 days?

2 Find out in detail about the experiments of Ingenhousz. Find out exactly what he did and how his results showed that light energy was involved in photosynthesis.

3 Who was Robert Hill? When did he do most of his scientific work? What did he discover about photosynthesis?

Test Yourself

7 Make a list of a) the reactants and b) the products of photosynthesis.

8 Explain why chlorophyll is placed below the arrow, rather than with the reactants and products.

Do plants respire?

Most people think that plants photosynthesise whereas animals respire. *This is completely wrong!!* *Both* plants *and* animals respire. However, plants are the only living things that can photosynthesise as well. So why do plants do both, and what is each process for?

Living things need food for energy. Plants make a food called glucose using photosynthesis. To get the energy out of glucose, both plants and animals respire:

> **glucose + oxygen → carbon dioxide + water + energy**

Plants respire all the time. This means they produce carbon dioxide and water. During the day, photosynthesis uses these products up before the plant can release them into the atmosphere. Photosynthesis then produces oxygen, which is used up in respiration. However, because photosynthesis happens more quickly than respiration for most of the day, oxygen is released into the atmosphere.

Test Yourself

9 Explain the difference between photosynthesis and respiration.

10 Which gas is released into the atmosphere by plants during the night? Is it produced by photosynthesis or respiration?

11 Plants make carbon dioxide all the time. Explain why carbon dioxide did not bubble up from the pondweed in the earlier experiment conducted in daylight.

What happens to glucose that is not respired?

Look at the tree in summer and winter in Figure 7. In the summer, there is lots of light and lots of photosynthesis can happen. In the winter there is not much light and so not much photosynthesis. The tree has to store food in the summer to feed itself later in the year. Trees aren't the only plants that store food for the winter. Look at the pictures of vegetables in Figure 8. Vegetables are the parts of the plant in which food is stored. The vegetables in the pictures store food in their roots, stem and leaves. Some plants also store food in their fruit. Glucose isn't just stored as starch. It can be turned into almost any of the other chemicals that a plant needs to stay alive.

a)

b)

Figure 7 ▲ A tree in a) summer and b) winter

99

Figure 8 ◄ Some different groups of vegetables

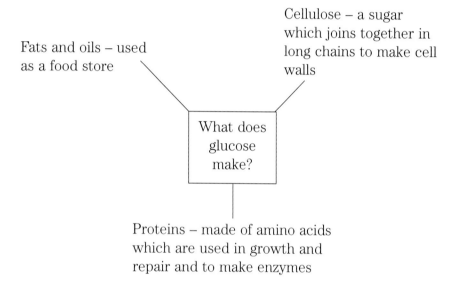

Fats and oils – used as a food store

Cellulose – a sugar which joins together in long chains to make cell walls

What does glucose make?

Proteins – made of amino acids which are used in growth and repair and to make enzymes

Test Yourself

12 Make a list of all the foods which can be made using glucose.

13 In what parts of a plant can food be stored?

So what about Aristotle?...

Was Aristotle completely wrong? Is any food absorbed through the roots? Well, photosynthesis is the only process that makes food for the plant. However, minerals are absorbed through the roots and may be added on to glucose to make proteins and other substances. Have a look in the next chapter to find out more about minerals.

Summary

When you have finished studying this chapter, you should understand that:

- ✔ Plants make glucose by a process called photosynthesis.

- ✔ Light energy in sunlight is used by chlorophyll in the leaves to make glucose.

- ✔ Photosynthesis also needs carbon dioxide and water.

- ✔ Photosynthesis produces oxygen as a waste product.

- ✔ The word equation for photosynthesis is:

- ✔ Plants release energy from glucose by respiration.

- ✔ Glucose that is not respired is stored or used for making new chemicals and tissues.

$$\text{carbon dioxide} + \text{water} \xrightarrow[\text{chlorophyll}]{\text{sunlight}} \text{glucose} + \text{oxygen}$$

End-of-Chapter Questions

1 Explain in your own words the following key terms you have met in this chapter:

photosynthesis

respiration

chlorophyll

2 Why does a plant on the windowsill lean towards the Sun?

3 Write down the word equations for photosynthesis and respiration. In what ways are they a) similar and b) different?

4 Plants need carbon dioxide to photosynthesise. Using what you know about respiration, suggest why plants will never run out of carbon dioxide.

5 The oxygen produced by photosynthesis is used by all living things. What is the name of the process that uses oxygen?

6 Name a plant that stores food in a) its stem, b) its roots and c) its leaves.

7 Global warming happens when too much carbon dioxide gets into the atmosphere. Global warming is a bad thing because it causes a rise in sea levels and may cause many animals and plants to go extinct. Using what you know about photosynthesis, explain why people are worried about the cutting down of the rainforests.

End-of-Chapter Questions continued

8 Look at the diagram of Jane's investigation. She moved the lamp closer and closer to her test tube and counted how many bubbles of oxygen were produced each minute by the pond weed. Her results are shown on the graph.

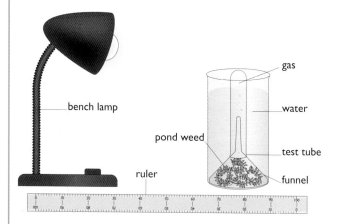

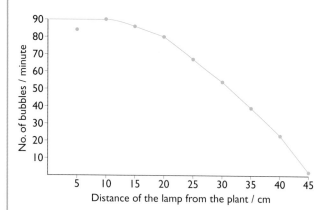

a) How many bubbles are produced when the lamp is 30 cm from the pond weed?

b) What does the graph show about the relationship between 'distance from the lamp' and 'number of bubbles produced per minute'?

c) Are there any results that do not fit the pattern? Can you think of a reason why?

d) Why was this not a fair test? (*Hint*: Think about what else the lamp gave off as well as light.)

e) With how many pieces of pondweed should she repeat the experiment at each distance from the lamp?

9 Look at the graphs that show the change in atmospheric oxygen and carbon dioxide levels in a forest over 24 hours.

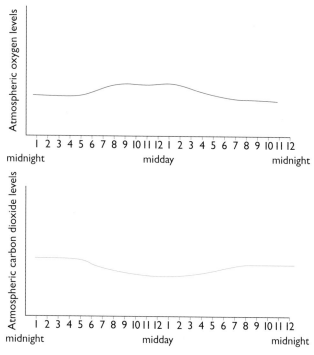

a) Explain why carbon dioxide levels decrease during the day.

b) Explain why oxygen levels decrease during the night.

10 *Photosynthesis* means *making food, using light*. But white light is made up of all the colours of the rainbow: red, orange, yellow, green, blue, indigo and violet. Devise an experiment to establish which colours of light are needed to make food. You should include a method, diagram and results table.

11 Using your school library and the Internet, investigate exactly how fruit and vegetable growers maximise the size and number of fruit they produce. How do their methods affect the rate at which photosynthesis happens in their crops?

10 Adaptations for photosynthesis

Every year, in villages across the country, there are thousands of competitions. Are they for the fastest runner, the brainiest boffin or the best football team? No. They are competitions for the biggest vegetables!

Large vegetables are packed with food, all of which has been made by photosynthesis. But why are plants good at photosynthesis? This chapter looks at how plants get the ingredients they need, how they move them to the leaves, and how they get them to take part in photosynthesis. As you will discover, almost every part of the plant has a role to play.

Where does water enter a plant?

Imagine you're an alien and you walk into someone's garden. You see someone watering the plants, and pouring water over the leaves. It starts to rain and water falls on the leaves. You may think that water enters the plant through the leaves. If this was true, a plant with its leaves permanently in water should grow very quickly. Look at the experiment in Figure 1. The plant with its leaves in water is dead. The plant with its roots in water is very healthy, suggesting that water enters a plant through its roots and not through its leaves.

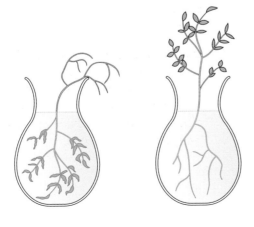

Figure 1 ◄ This experiment shows us that water enters the plant through the roots, not the leaves

How does water enter the plant and travel up to the leaves?

Plant roots have special features that help them to absorb a lot of water. Look at the drawing of the roots in Figure 2. They do not go straight down, but branch off sideways. Each branch gives the plant access to a new supply of water. From each branch, there are other tiny branches called root hairs. These are extensions of cells in the root, and they increase the **surface area** of the root. This means that the root has more of its surface touching water in the soil. Because of this, the root can absorb more water more quickly.

Figure 2 ◀ The structure of a root

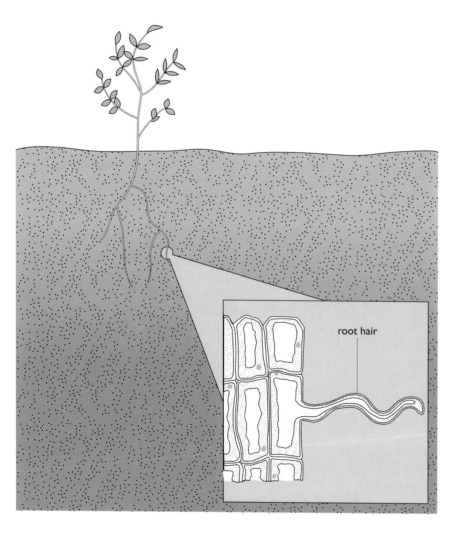

root hair

Once the water has been absorbed, it needs to be transported up to the leaves. If you were designing a transport system to pump water around your house, you would probably use pipes or tubes. Tubes (arteries, veins and capillaries) carry blood around your body. They are part of your body's **vascular system**. To find out if a plant has a vascular system, we will need to cut it open and look inside.

Extension box

Preparing a section

To look inside a plant, scientists cannot shrink themselves down very small and walk in. They must cut the plant open. Imagine we were interested in the contents of a plant's stem. We could cut the stem in two different directions: across the stem and along the stem. When you cut across the stem, we say you are cutting a **transverse section** (cross section). When you cut along the stem, we say you are cutting a **longitudinal section**.

If you get hold of a plant stem and cut across it, all you can see is green tissue. If you want to have a look at the inside of the stem in more detail, you need to use a microscope. However, you would need to make your specimen thin enough for light to pass through it. To do this, you need to cut a very thin slice from the stem. This is easily done using a special machine called a microtome. This can cut slices thinner than 1 mm thick.

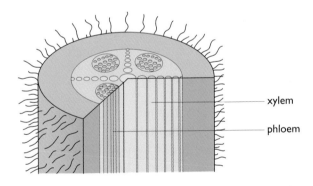

Figure 3 ▲ A section through a root

Look at the cross-section of a plant's roots in Figure 3. The drawing shows how the picture relates to what the root is actually like inside. You can see the long tubes that run from one end of the root to the other. Both types of tube are made of cells lined up end to end.

- The **phloem** tubes carry sugar around the plant.
- The **xylem** vessels are tubes that carry water around the plant. They are tough and hard because their walls have been filled with a chemical called lignin.

If the roots have a vascular system, it should come as no surprise that the stem also has a vascular system (see Figure 4). Again, phloem tubes carry sugar away from the leaves, and xylem vessels carry water from the roots to the leaves.

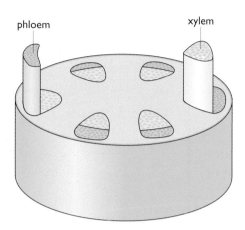

Figure 4 ▲   A section through a stem

Ideas and Evidence

Scientists discovered that the xylem transports water and the phloem transports sugar using a series of simple experiments.

Xylem

★ They placed a cut piece of celery in a beaker of red ink and left it for 24 hours. They knew that the water and the ink from the beaker had moved up the stem because it had entered the leaves and they had turned red. When they cut the stem, they discovered that the ink was only in the xylem vessels, suggesting that the water and ink are transported through the xylem.

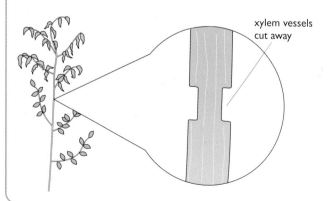

xylem vessels cut away

★ When they cut away the xylem vessels half way up the stem of a plant, the leaves above the cut wilted, suggesting the flow of water had been blocked. In contrast, the leaves below the cut were still healthy.

Phloem

★ If you put a plant in a jar with radioactive carbon dioxide, eventually the plant uses the gas to make sugar. When that sugar is transported around the plant, you can monitor where it goes. When scientists did this, they found the sugar moving through the phloem and they never found it in the xylem.

Find out:

1   Find out what the cells look like which make up xylem and phloem. Draw a picture of each and describe their main features.

2   Find out what else is transported around the plant in the phloem.

Extension box

The transpiration stream

But why does water move through the roots and up the stem? It seems odd that it can flow upwards against gravity. The answer is that water is constantly being evaporated from holes in the leaves called **stomata** (singular: stoma). Look at the picture. The condensation on the inside of the bag is water that has been lost from the leaves. Water moves up the plant to replace the water that has been evaporated. This stream of water moving up the plant is called the **transpiration stream**.

Test Yourself

1 Copy one of the root hair cells from Figure 3 and label the parts of the cell.

2 Explain why increasing the surface area of the root is helpful to the plant.

3 When do you lose water more quickly by sweating: on a hot day or a cold day?

4 If you put a stick of celery in a hot room, would the red ink move up the stem more quickly or more slowly than if you put it in a cold room?

5 When you eat celery, the chewy tough part is the xylem vessels. What chemical makes the xylem chewy and tough?

How is the leaf adapted to carry out photosynthesis?

Look at the picture of the leaves in Figure 5. They look very simple, but in fact the leaf is one of the most specialised organs you will find in a plant. Remember, the leaf is made of cells and photosynthesis happens inside some of those cells. Simply by looking at the outside of the leaf, we can begin to understand how the leaf is **adapted** for photosynthesis. However, just like in the stem and root, we can understand more if we have a look inside the leaf. We can do this by cutting the leaf across the middle and having a look at the cut end using a microscope (see Figure 6). Inside the leaf are lots of different tissues. The tissues tend to be in layers, which you can see labelled down the left hand side of the drawing. Each tissue has a different job.

Figure 5 ▲ The external features of a typical leaf

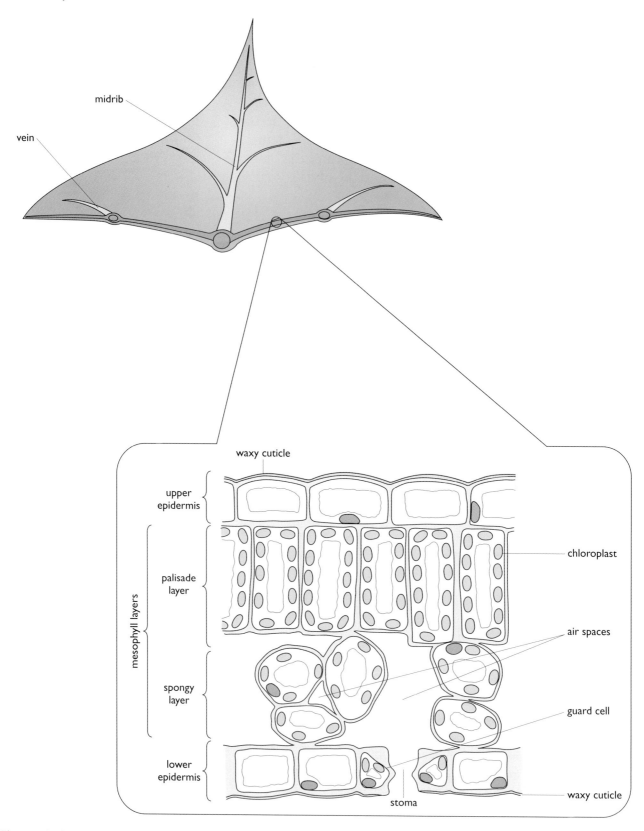

midrib

vein

waxy cuticle

upper epidermis

mesophyll layers

palisade layer

chloroplast

spongy layer

air spaces

guard cell

lower epidermis

stoma

waxy cuticle

Figure 6 ▲   The internal structure of a leaf

Upper epidermis

1 Protects the top surface of the leaf.
2 Makes a waxy cuticle, which is waterproof and stops the leaf losing too much water.
3 Is clear (not green) so that light can pass straight through and reach the layers below.

Palisade layer

1 Contains chloroplasts, which contain chlorophyll.
2 Chlorophyll catches light energy from the Sun.
3 Cells are packed tightly together so as much light as possible is captured by the chloroplasts.

Spongy layer

1 If any light travels straight through the palisade layer, chloroplasts in the spongy layer may absorb it.
2 There are large air spaces between the cells to allow gases to travel in and out.

Lower epidermis

1 Protects the underside of the leaf.
2 There are holes or stomata between the cells. These let gases in and out of the leaf.

Vascular bundle

1 Contains phloem tubes, which carry glucose away from the leaf to the rest of the plant.
2 Contains xylem vessels, which carry water from the stem to the cells that need it for photosynthesis.

The stomata and the air spaces inside the leaf allow oxygen, carbon dioxide and water vapour to travel in and out of the leaf. Just like in humans, an exchange of gases of this kind is called **gaseous exchange**. During the day, carbon dioxide enters the leaf cells and oxygen leaves the leaf cells. During the night, the opposite happens.

Test Yourself

6 Explain why leaves are a) thin, b) broad and c) green.

7 Which two layers of cells inside the leaf can photosynthesise?

8 What is the role of the stomata?

9 What is gaseous exchange?

Why does the leaf let water out?

Water is needed by all living things and can be quite precious. Many plants have special adaptations to stop themselves losing too much water. The cacti in Figure 7 have spines instead of broad leaves to minimise water loss through the leaves.

So why do most plants have stomata through which water can escape? After all, wouldn't it be better not to lose any water at all? Well, there must be some way for carbon dioxide and oxygen to go in and out of the leaf as part of photosynthesis. The fact that water evaporates as well may just be an accident. However, the loss of water from the leaves is useful to the plant for another reason.

When water is lost from the leaves, water from the roots and stem moves up to fill the space. Dissolved in this water are minerals which are essential to a plant's survival, and which need to be delivered to all parts of the plant. Like water, minerals are absorbed by the roots and travel in the xylem. When water moves upwards, it sweeps along any dissolved minerals as well.

You may know about minerals already. Fertilisers are packed with minerals, which is why farmers and gardeners give them to their plants. Magnesium is a mineral in fertiliser which helps the plant to make chlorophyll. Look at Figure 8. You can see the difference in the plant after it has been given some fertiliser containing magnesium.

Figure 7 ▲ Cacti are specially adapted to live in areas where there is little water

a) Plant lacking magnesium   b) Plant once fertiliser has been added

Figure 8 ▲ Magnesium is essential for a healthy plant

Look at Table 1 to see why plants need other minerals.

Mineral	What is its job?	What happens if the plant does not get enough?
Nitrogen (nitrate)	Making leaves	Not much growth, pale leaves, weak stems

Potassium (potash)	Making flowers	Brown leaves, low yield of fruit, low disease resistance

Phosphorus (phosphate)	Making roots	Short roots and stems, small purple leaves, low yield of fruit

Table 1 ▲

Test Yourself

10 Draw a plant that has not got enough magnesium and nitrogen.

11 Draw a plant that has not got enough phosphorus and potassium.

Ideas and Evidence

Scientists discovered that minerals were carried in the xylem using two pieces of evidence.

1 They used a syringe and inserted the needle into some xylem vessels. When they sucked out the liquid inside, they found it contained minerals.

2 They gave a plant water which contained radioactive minerals. When they removed the xylem and phloem from the plant after several hours, the xylem was radioactive and the phloem was not.

Summary

When you have finished studying this chapter, you should understand that:

✔ Plants can store food in their stem, roots and leaves.

✔ All the organs in a plant have different jobs.

✔ Water enters a plant through the roots.

✔ Root hairs increase the surface area of the roots for absorption of water.

✔ Phloem tubes carry sugar around the plant and xylem vessels carry water and minerals around the plant.

✔ The internal structure of the leaf is adapted for gaseous exchange and photosynthesis.

✔ Plants need minerals in order to stay healthy.

End-of-Chapter Questions

1 Explain in your own words the following key terms you have met in this chapter:

surface area

vascular system

transverse section

longitudinal section

phloem

xylem

stomata

transpiration stream

adaptations

gaseous exchange

2 What do a) xylem and b) phloem carry around the plant?

3 Some plant cells do not contain chloroplasts.

    a) Why do the cells in the upper epidermis of a leaf contain no chloroplasts?

    b) Why do cells in plant roots contain no chloroplasts?

4 Look at the graph. It shows the speed at which red ink flows up the xylem vessels in a stick of celery when the celery is placed in different temperatures.

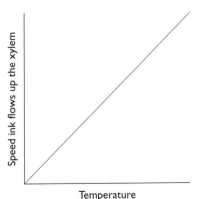

    a) As the temperature increases, what happens to the speed at which the ink flows up the xylem?

    b) By thinking about how quickly washing dries on a hot day and on a cold day, explain the results of the experiment.

The experimenter placed the celery on a balance to monitor the mass of the plant during the experiment.

    c) She found that it remained constant until the beaker was empty. After this the mass of the plant began to drop. Explain this observation.

She also did the experiment on two different plants. Plant A had roots with lots of root hairs. Plant B had roots with very few root hairs. She watered both with water containing red ink. After one hour she cut the stem of each plant near the top and examined the cut end for red ink.

    d) The red ink had reached the top of the stem in Plant A, but not in Plant B. Explain why.

Finally she did the experiment on two other plants. Plant C had broad leaves and Plant D had narrow leaves. After one hour she cut the stem of each plant near the top and examined the cut end for red ink.

    e) The red ink had reached the top of the stem in Plant C, but not in Plant D. Explain why.

    f) Explain why a cactus plant has very narrow spiny leaves.

5 In your digestive system, food particles are absorbed into the blood. How does your digestive system increase the surface area across which this can happen?

6 A technology company wants to design solar panels with which to generate electricity. Solar panels are made of lots of photovoltaic cells, which make electricity when light hits them. Using what you know about leaves, design a solar panel that will generate electricity as efficiently as possible.

7 Design a fertiliser for raspberry bushes. You must decide which minerals will be in your fertiliser and how much of each mineral you will use. Your advert should include all relevant scientific information and should fill one side of A4 paper.

Variation and inheritance

Some living things look very different. There is a lot of **variation** between them.

Some living things look more similar to each other.

Some living things look even more similar. Look at the boy and his father. You can see the likeness. There is little variation between them.

Some living things are almost identical. These 'identical twins' are almost exactly the same. There is almost no variation between them.

This chapter will help you to understand why there is variation between living things, and how that variation is caused. It will even help you to work out why you look a little like other members of your family.

Variation between species and within species

Members of different **species** look very different to one another. A cat looks very different to a snake. An oak tree looks very different to a rose bush. Variation between species is called **interspecific variation**.

Even though animals and plants in the same species look very similar, there is also variation between them. We call this **intraspecific variation**.

But how do we know if living things are in the same species or in different species? Scientists usually group living things into the same species if they look very similar to one another. However, it is sometimes difficult to judge how similar two individuals are. You look slightly different to all of the people in the pictures above, and yet you are in the same species. Because of this, scientists usually group living things into the same species if they can reproduce together to produce fertile offspring.

Test Yourself

1 What is the difference between interspecific variation and intraspecific variation?

2 How do scientists decide if two individuals are in the same species?

How can we describe variation?

Variation can be described in lots of different ways. You could write a description for a guide book, or make up a table to describe particular species (see Table 1).

	legs	beak	wings	tail
How many?	2	1	2	1
What colour?	pink	red	black and white	black and white
How long?	5 cm	4 cm	15 cm	22 cm

Table 1 ▲   Describing the buffalo weaver bird of Southern Africa

Most scientists tend to draw graphs of variation. Aisha collected information from her class at Southgate School. Look at the tally chart and the graph she drew, showing how the eye colour of her class varies.

	tally	total
blue	卌 卌	10
brown	卌 |||	8
green	卌		6

Danny was in the same class, and decided to collect information about how the height of his class varies. Look at the tally chart and graph that he drew.

	tally	total
140.0–144.9	||	2
145.0–149.9	||	2
150.0–154.9	卌		6
155.0–159.9	卌		6
160.0–164.9	||||	4
165.0–169.9	|||	3
170.0–174.9		0
175.0–179.9			1

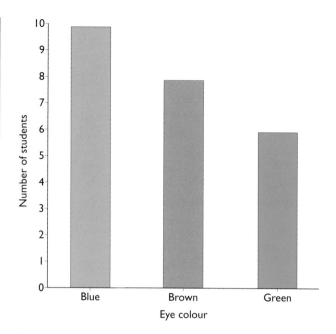

Figure 1 ▲ Aisha's bar chart of results

Figure 2 ◄ Danny's histogram of results

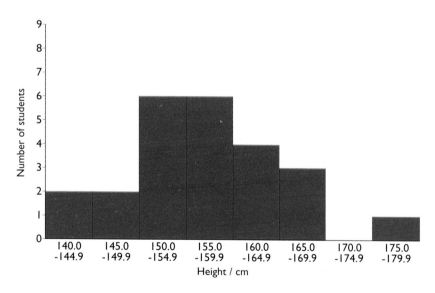

The two graphs show examples of two different kinds of variation.

- Height is an example of **continuous variation**. Students can be *any* height between a maximum height and a minimum height. Because of this, Danny had to make up his own artificial groups before he could draw the graph.

- Eye colour is an example of **discontinuous variation**. Eye colour falls into natural groups with no intermediates. The students either have brown, blue or green eyes.

Test Yourself

3   Is body mass an example of continuous or discontinuous variation?

4   Some people can roll their tongues. Other people cannot roll their tongues. Is this an example of continuous or discontinuous variation?

5   Draw a graph of one continuously varying feature from the animals below.

6   Draw a graph of one discontinuously varying feature from the animals below.

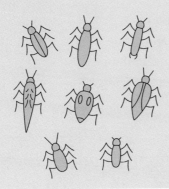

Inherited variation

You may have been told that you look like your father or mother. This is because you **inherit** features from both of your parents. Look at the family in Figure 3. The boy has inherited his big nose and blonde hair from his mother, and his big ears and green eyes from his father.

Figure 3 ◄ You can see that this boy has inherited features from both parents

But how do you inherit features? Your features are controlled by **genes**. Variation caused by genes is called **genetic variation**. Genes are the instructions inside the nucleus of each of your cells.

These instructions originally came from your mother and father. Think back to when your life began. A sperm cell from your father joined together with an egg cell from your mother. The cell produced (the **zygote**) received half of its genes from its mother, and half from its father. The zygote then divided lots of times until it produced you: a new human being. Every time a cell divides, it puts an exact copy of its genes into each of its daughter cells. That means that each cell in your body contains a full set of genes, half from your mother, and half from your father.

But what happens if the genes you inherit from each parent are different? Imagine you inherited a gene for blue eyes from your father, and a gene for brown eyes from your mother. What colour would your eyes be? In this case, the gene for brown eyes is stronger than the gene for blue eyes, and your eyes would be brown. We say the gene for brown eyes is **dominant** to the gene for blue eyes, which is **recessive**. Different versions of particular genes are either dominant or recessive. The versions of genes that you inherit determine what you look like.

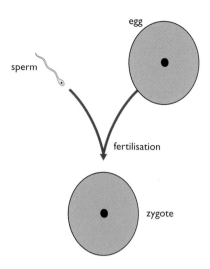

Figure 4 ▲ Fertilisation

Ideas and Evidence

The work of Gregor Mendel

Gregor Mendel was a monk who lived in Czechoslovakia in the 19th Century. He was interested in how pea plants inherited their characteristics. His work forms the basis of what we now know about dominant and recessive genes.

To investigate the inheritance of stem length, he transferred pollen from the anthers of a dwarf plant to the stigma of a tall plant. He found that all of the seeds produced tall plants. He realised that 'tall' was dominant to 'dwarf'. That means that 'tall' was somehow stronger than 'dwarf'.

After Mendel had grown the seeds, and they had produced flowers, he transferred the pollen from the anthers of one of these tall plants to a stigma on one of the other tall plants. He grew the seeds that were produced.

For every three tall plants, there was also a dwarf plant.

Mendel did not know what genes were; they had not yet been discovered. But he did realise that each plant gave a 'factor' to its children, and that every plant had a pair of factors. He gave his factors letters to explain his ideas. A tall factor was given a letter T and a dwarf factor was given a letter t.

Mendel tried to gain recognition for his work from other scientists. However, because he was a monk, they did not really think he was worth listening to. He did not help himself, because he published his work in a journal which very few scientists read. It was only 35 years after his death that people began to realise the importance of his work.

Genes are not alone in the nucleus. They are actually linked together in long chains called **chromosomes**. You can see some chromosomes in Figure 5.

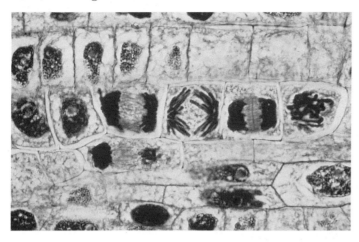

Figure 5 ◄ The chromosomes are visible in these root cells

You already know that genes come in pairs, and that one gene comes from your mother and one gene comes from your father. Because genes are on chromosomes, chromosomes must also come in pairs. One chromosome of each pair comes from your mother, and one chromosome of each pair comes from your father. Inside the nucleus of each cell in your body, there are 23 pairs of chromosomes: 46 chromosomes altogether.

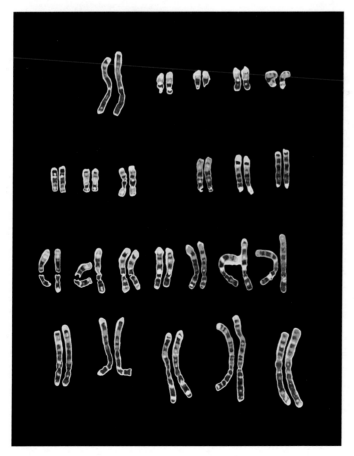

Figure 6 ◄ Humans have 23 pairs of chromosomes

Extension box

What are genes and chromosomes made of?

Chromosomes and their genes are made of a chemical called deoxyribonucleic acid (DNA). The structure of DNA was discovered by James Watson and Francis Crick at the Cavendish Laboratory at the University of Cambridge in 1953. They won the Nobel Prize for their work, which they published in the journal *Nature*.

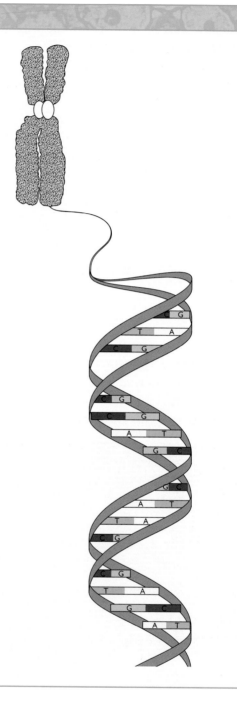

You can see what DNA looks like in detail in the picture. The DNA itself is in two strands which wind around each other. The order of the letters determines what the gene does.

Test Yourself

7   What do genes do?

8   How do you inherit genes from your mother and father?

9   How many chromosomes are in one of your skin cells?

Environmental variation

Identical twins have exactly the same genes because they come from a single fertilised egg or zygote. Instead of forming one new baby, the zygote splits into two cells which each develop into a new baby. Figure 7 shows how identical twins are formed. Because they have identical genes, you would expect identical twins to be absolutely identical. This isn't completely true. There is often still variation between them. Identical twins do not look identical because they have different lifestyles. They may eat different things, they may do different amounts of exercise, and they may dress and style their hair differently. They should be identical but they look different. This type of variation is called **environmental variation**. Because environmental variation only changes your characteristics and not your genes, it cannot be inherited by your children.

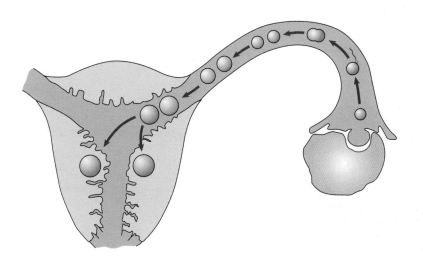

Figure 7 ◄ When the egg is fertilised it splits into two separate cells. Each of these forms an embryo, which implants into the wall of the uterus and grows into a baby

Most of your features are actually affected by both genes and the environment.

- You may have a gene for intelligence, but you will not be intelligent unless you go to school.
- You may have a gene for being tall, but you will not be tall unless you have a balanced diet
- You may have a gene for blonde hair, but you will not have blonde hair if you dye it red!

Some features are controlled only by genes. These include blood group, natural eye colour and natural hair colour.

10 Which of these are affected by both genes and the environment?

  a) Mass
  b) Height
  c) Blood group
  d) Eye colour
  e) Intelligence

11 For the factors that you have identified in Question 10, explain how environmental variation affects them.

Selective breeding in animals

Selective breeding happens when humans decide which animals or plants to breed together. Look at the different breeds of dogs in Figure 8. They look completely different, but they are members of the same species; they can breed together. They look different because humans have used selective breeding to develop certain characteristics.

Figure 8 ◄ These dogs are members of the same species, but they have been bred to look and act differently

So how does selective breeding work? Imagine you are a sheep farmer. You want the sheep to produce high quality wool. Choose a male and female that both have high quality wool. Put them in a pen together and let them mate. When the 'children' have grown up, some of them are likely to have high quality wool. This is because they have inherited the genes for high quality wool from their parents. To produce even more animals with high quality wool, you should keep selecting the sheep with the best quality wool and breed them together over many generations.

Selective breeding has been used to produce animals with particular desired characteristics for hundreds of years. Look at the pictures of huskies, greyhounds and sheepdogs. The huskies have been bred for strength, the greyhounds for speed and the sheepdogs for intelligence.

a) A sheepdog

b) A husky

c) A greyhound

Figure 9 ◄

Selective breeding can also be used to produce attractive animals for pets, and to produce farm animals that produce lots of meat, milk or wool.

123

Ideas and Evidence — Artificial insemination

Sometimes a male and female animal may not be willing to breed together. Another way to carry out selective breeding is to obtain some sperm from the male and place it directly into the vagina of the female. This is called artificial insemination and is often used for breeding cattle. Because you can freeze the sperm taken from a bull, it means you can keep it for long periods of time and still use it when it is needed.

Test Yourself

12 Why do farmers carry out selective breeding?

13 Write down how you would use selective breeding to produce large cattle.

Selective breeding in plants

Selective breeding in plants happens in exactly the same way. You choose plants with particular desired characteristics and breed them together. Fruit and vegetables have been bred to look nice or to taste nice. Houseplants and garden plants have been bred to look pretty. Crop plants have been bred to have large grains. Imagine you have two wheat plants that have characteristics you want to combine into one plant:

1 Plant A has large grains but a weak stem.
2 Plant B has small grains but a strong stem.

To produce a plant with large grains and a strong stem, you must breed plant A and plant B together. This will produce some plants that have inherited the gene for having large grains *and* the gene for having a strong stem. It is important to realise that because some genes are recessive, you may need to keep choosing the best plants over many generations before all the desired characteristics are combined into one plant. You must also be careful of some added complications:

- Plants will not breed together without a little help. To make sure that pollen from one plant reaches the stigma of another, you must transfer it yourself. Breeders often use a paintbrush to do this.
- Unwanted pollen from other flowers may reach the stigma. To prevent this, you can put the plant inside a plastic bag before breeding.

Extension box

What is genetic engineering?

Selective breeding is a way of combining desired genes in particular animals or plants, so they show the characteristics you want. However, selective breeding can take a lot of time. It often requires several generations of breeding before you produce an individual with all of the desired characteristics.

Genetic engineering does the same job as selective breeding, but in less time. Genetic engineers take a plant with the desired characteristic and find the gene that controls that characteristic inside the nucleus of its cells. They cut the gene out using enzymes and insert it into a new plant without that characteristic.

Genetic engineering has already been used to improve crops. Scientists have inserted a gene into tomato plants which slows down how quickly they rot. Maize plants have also been genetically engineered so they are more resistant to insects and disease.

Test Yourself

14 Give three reasons why plant breeders use selective breeding.

15 What are the problems with selective breeding in plants.

Summary

When you have finished studying this chapter, you should understand that:

- Variation between species is called interspecific variation.

- Variation within a species is called intraspecific variation.

- Living things are said to be in the same species if they can breed together to produce fertile young.

- There are two types of variation within a species: continuous variation and discontinuous variation.

- Variation can be inherited (genetic). This occurs because there are genes from your parents in the egg and sperm. When these fuse, the zygote receives information from each parent, which will control the new baby's characteristics.

- Variation can also be environmental. This occurs because of differences in lifestyles, such as eating habits.

- Selective breeding is when humans decide which animals or plants to breed together to get particular characteristics, for example large grains in wheat plants or thick wool in sheep.

End-of-Chapter Questions

1 Explain in your own words the following key terms you have met in this chapter:

variation

species

interspecific variation

intraspecific variation

continuous variation

discontinuous variation

inherit

genes

genetic variation

zygote

dominant

recessive

chromosomes

environmental variation

selective breeding

2 If you train hard in the gym, the size of your muscles increases. Explain why your children will not automatically have big muscles because of this.

3 Jack has collected data about finger length in his classmates.

Name	Finger length
John	5.0
Jane	6.3
Freddie	4.8
Aysha	6.3
Jaysh	5.2
Gbemi	5.5
Lee	5.5
Kim	6.0
Yip	5.7
Hok	5.2
Geoff	5.5
Mark	5.5
Mathew	5.9
Luke	5.8
Sally	6.1
Jo	5.6
Helen	5.6
Richard	5.1
Brian	5.3
Barrie	5.3

a) Draw a graph using this data.

b) Write down whether this variation is continuous or discontinuous.

4 Why do humans have two versions of every gene?

5 Hannah has two versions of the eye colour gene: green and blue. Blue is recessive to green. What colour are Hannah's eyes?

6 Horses are bred to run fast in races. Suggest why horses that have been bred in this way may not always run fast.

7 Write an instruction manual for a plant breeder who wants to use selective breeding to increase the fruit yield on her strawberry plants.

8 Jaysh and her partner both have brown eyes. They have a child with blue eyes. Explain why.

12 Classification

Look at the music bands in the pictures. If you were to describe them, you would probably call Westlife a 'boy band', Motorhead a 'heavy metal' band, and the Dubliners a 'folk band'. When you give them these names, you are putting them into groups.

- Westlife, and lots of other boy bands, are in the 'boy band' group.
- Motorhead, and lots of other heavy metal bands, are in the 'heavy metal' group.

- The Dubliners, and lots of other folk bands, are in the 'folk band' group.

Putting things into groups is called **classifying**. Humans are always putting things into groups. Think about pencils and pens. They look very similar, but are classified into two separate groups. Pens are classified in a different group to pencils because they contain ink.

Scientists are just like anyone else – they like to put living things into groups. Scientists put living things into the same group if they have a lot of features in common. These groups are called taxonomic groups because the scientific name for classification is **taxonomy**. One example of a taxonomic group is a **species**. A species is a group whose members have a large number of features in common, and can reproduce together to produce fertile offspring. This chapter looks at how scientists classify living things, and why it is important to do so.

Why do scientists classify living things?

Scientists put living things into groups for several different reasons:

- It helps them put living things into order, making them easier to think about.
- It helps them to understand more about a living thing they have never met before. Imagine if you met the animal in Figure 1. You may put it into the same group as lions and cheetahs, and realise that you should probably run away very fast!

Figure 1 ◄ If you met this animal, you would probably run!

- It makes it easier to tell other scientists about a living thing. If everyone in the world classifies pens and pencils in the same way, everyone would understand what something looks like and how it works if you called it a pencil.
- It makes it easier to work out how closely related two species are. If the species have a lot in common, they are likely to be closely related.

Test Yourself

1   What is taxonomy?

2   Why does classifying help scientists to tell other scientists about a living thing?

How do scientists classify living things?

Every living thing is in a group called a **kingdom**. There are five kingdoms: plants, animals, fungi, protoctistans and prokaryotes. Each member of each kingdom has features in common with other members of the kingdom.

Ideas and Evidence

Classifying into kingdoms

Scientists have been putting living things into groups for hundreds of years. Around 350BC, Aristotle, a Greek philosopher, decided there were two main groups of living things: animals and plants. According to Aristotle, plants were green and animals moved.

In the 19th Century, John Hogg said there were three main groups: animals, plants and microbes. Microbes were any living things that could only be seen using a microscope.

In the 20th Century, living things were divided into five groups called kingdoms. The scientist who came up with the five kingdoms was called Robert Whittaker. Lynn Margulis and Karlene Schwartz refined and published his ideas in a book called *Five kingdoms: an illustrated guide to the phyla of life on earth.*

All the living things in a kingdom are divided into groups called phyla (singular: **phylum**), according to how many features they have in common. In a similar way, all the living things in a phylum are divided into groups called classes, according to how many features they have in common. Each **class** is then divided up into orders; each **order** is divided up into families; each **family** is divided up into genera; and each **genus** (the singular of genera) is divided up into **species**.

You can draw this diagram as a venn diagram (Figure 2) or as a branching tree (Figure 3). This is the most common way of showing how different groups are divided up.

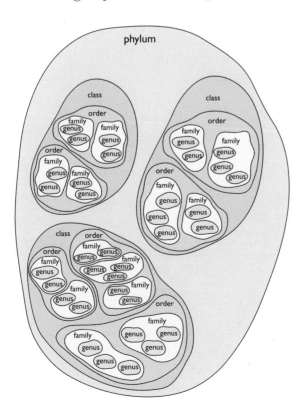

Figure 2 ◄ One way of representing how Kingdoms are divided

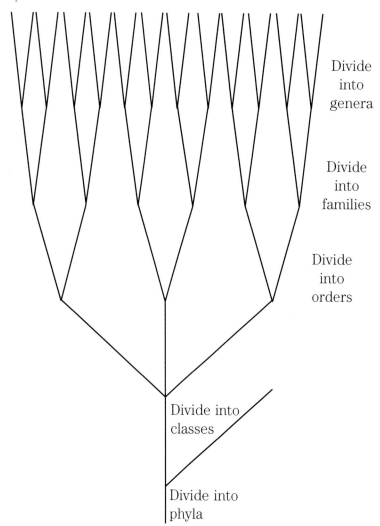

Divide
into
genera

Divide
into
families

Divide
into
orders

Divide into
classes

Divide into
phyla

Figure 3 ◄ The branching tree method of dividing up the Kingdoms

The names of each of these groups are difficult to remember. Try using this rhyme to help.

Kingdom	**K**inky
Phylum	**P**igs
Class	**C**an
Order	**O**nly
Family	**F**ly
Genus	**G**oing
Species	**S**ideways

Look at how the system can be used to classify a human.

Kingdom	Animals
Phylum	Chordates
Class	Mammals
Order	Primates
Family	Hominids
Genus	*Homo*
Species	*sapiens*

Classifying species

Carl Linnaeus was the father of modern classification. He was Swedish and lived between 1707 and 1778. He was the first person to classify living things into a genus and a species according to how similar they looked. He gave each species a two part Latin name. The Latin name for humans is *Homo sapiens*. Homo is the name of our genus and sapiens is the name of our species. You always put Latin names in italics or, if you are writing by hand, you underline them. Every scientist in the world still uses these names. By using the Latin name, scientists who speak different languages can be certain they are talking about the same species.

Test Yourself

3   How many kingdoms of living things are there?

4   A phylum is divided into several smaller groups. What is the name of these groups?

5   An order is divided into several smaller groups. What is the name of these groups?

6   Why are humans in a different order to horses and zebras?

Classification of animals

Animals are living things that are made of lots of cells and feed on other living things. They all have a nervous system and can usually move.

Invertebrates

Look at Table 1 to see some of the **invertebrate** phyla. Invertebrates are animals that do not have a backbone.

	Characteristics	Example
Cnidarians	• Simple, sac-like body • Tentacles and stinging cells • Live in water	

	Characteristics	Example
Annelids	<ul><li>Long body which is divided into rings</li><li>Hairs called chaetae which help in movement</li><li>Live in water and on land</li></ul>	
Molluscs	<ul><li>Soft body covered by a shell</li><li>Large muscular foot</li><li>Live in water and on land</li></ul>	
Echinoderms	<ul><li>Star-shaped body covered by spines and hard skin</li><li>Live in water</li></ul>	
Arthropods	<ul><li>Jointed legs</li><li>Hard, outside skeleton</li><li>Live in water and on land</li></ul>	

Table 1 ▲   Characteristics of some invertebrate phyla

The arthropods are actually an enormous phylum of animals, which we usually divide up into classes. You can see some of those classes in Table 2.

	Characteristics	Examples
Insects	• Body divided into three sections • Six jointed legs • Antennae • Many have two pairs of wings	
Crustaceans	• Very hard outside skeleton • Two pairs of antennae	
Myriapods	• Long bodies divided into lots of sections • Each section has one or two pairs of jointed legs • Antennae	
Arachnids	• Body divided into two sections • Eight jointed legs • No antennae	

Table 2 ▲ Characteristics of some anthropod classes

Vertebrates

Animals with backbones are called **vertebrates**. There is only one vertebrate phylum: the chordates. Table 3 shows you how the chordates are divided up into classes.

	Characteristics	Examples
Fish	• Gills, scales and fins • Streamlined body • Live in water	
Amphibians	• Lungs • Smooth, wet skin • Live in water and on land • Eggs laid in water	
Reptiles	• Lungs • Skin covered in tough, dry scales • Live in water or on land • Eggs have a rubbery shell and are laid on land	
Birds	• Lungs and beak • Feathers and wings • Lay eggs with a hard shell • Keep their body temperature constant	
Mammals	• Body covered in hair or fur • Babies usually develop inside mother • Babies fed on milk from the mother • Keep their body temperature constant	

Table 3 ▲ Characteristics of the chordates

7   Which phylum of animals has a large muscular foot?

8   Which two classes of animals keep their body temperature constant?

9   Make a list of the characteristics of a millipede.

Classification of plants

Plants are living things that are made of lots of cells and contain the green pigment chlorophyll. They use chlorophyll to make food by photosynthesis. Plants are classified into four main groups. Look at Table 4 to see what the members of each group have in common.

	Characteristics	Examples
Mosses and liverworts	• Small plants with no flowers and tiny roots. • Reproduce using spores. • Live in damp, shady places.	
Ferns	• Plants with leaves called fronds and no flowers. • Reproduce using spores. • Live in damp places.	
Conifers	• Large plants with no flowers. • Reproduce using seeds, which are made inside cones. • Live in a variety of places.	
Flowering plants	• Plants that have flowers. • Reproduce using seeds, which are made inside fruit. • Live in a wide variety of places.	

Table 4 ▲   Characteristics of different plant groups

Extension box

Classification of other kingdoms

Prokaryotes

Prokaryotes can only be seen with a microscope. They are made of one cell which has a wall but no nucleus. Some prokaryotes can make their own food by photosynthesis. Others feed saprophytically. This means they release enzymes to digest food outside their bodies and then absorb it through their cell wall.

Protoctistans

Protoctistans include single-celled organisms, and simple many-celled organisms. Their cells have a nucleus and are easily visible using a microscope. Some feed by absorbing food through their cell membrane. Others can make their own food by photosynthesis.

Fungi

Fungi are made of many cells arranged in fine threads called hyphae in a complex network called a mycelium. The threads may be separate, or woven together to form mushrooms. Fungi used to be classified as plants, however fungi cannot make their own food. They feed saprophytically like some prokaryotes.

Test Yourself

10 Which plants have no flowers and tiny roots?

11 Which plants produce seeds inside fruit?

12 Which plants reproduce using spores?

Identifying living things

If you look on your school field or in your local park, you will see lots of different species of plants. Each of those plants has a name, but how can you find out what they are called? You could use a field guide, but you would have to go through it page by page until you found the correct plant. Instead you could use a key. Keys are written by scientists to help you identify plants and animals. Look at the key in Figure 4. You can use it to identify the flowers in the picture. Unfortunately, if you have a lot of flowers, this type of key can take up a lot of room. Because of this, we tend to re-write it as a question key or numbered key (Figure 5).

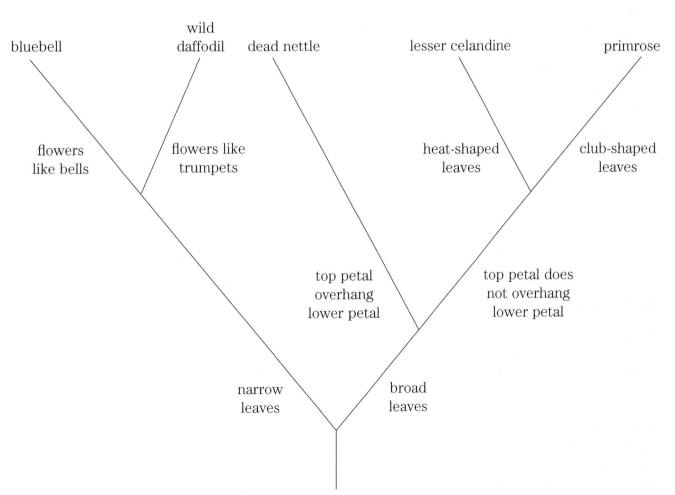

Figure 4 ▲ A branching key

| **1** leaves narrow | go to 2 |
| leaves broad | go to 3 |

| **2** flowers like bells | bluebell |
| flower like trumpet | wild daffodil |

| **3** top petal overhangs lower petal | dead nettle |
| top peteal does not overhang lower petal | go to 4 |

| **4** leaf heart-shaped | lesser celandine |
| leaf club-shaped | primrose |

Figure 5 ▲ A numbered key

Test Yourself

13 Use the key below to identify the drawing of the insect.

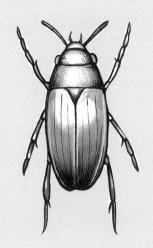

1 Does it have legs? If the answer is YES then go to question 2.
   If the answer is NO then go to question 3.

2 Does it have six legs? If the answer is YES then go to question 4.
   If the answer is NO then it is a WATER LOUSE.

3 Does it have a segmented body? If the answer is YES then it is a LEECH.
   If the answer is no then it is a FLATWORM.

4 Are the front legs longer than the rest? If the answer is YES then it is a WATER SCORPION.
   If the answer is NO then it is a WATER BEETLE.

Summary

When you have finished studying this chapter, you should understand that:

✔ Scientists classify living things.

✔ Living things are divided into five kingdoms: animals, plants, prokaryotes, protoctistans and fungi.

✔ Kingdoms are divided into smaller groups including phyla, classes, orders, families, genera and species.

✔ Animals and plants have different characteristics and what these characteristics are.

✔ Invertebrates and vertebrates are different and can be classified into smaller groups.

✔ Plants can be classified into smaller groups.

✔ Keys can be used to identify living things.

End-of-Chapter Questions

1 Explain in your own words the following key terms you have met in this chapter:

classify

taxonomy

kingdom

phylum

class

order

family

genus

species

invertebrate

vertebrate

2 For each of the following animals, write down which phylum they are in: a) human, b) lizard, c) housefly and d) starfish.

3 For each of the following animals, write down which class they are in: a) human, b) bird, c) housefly and d) lobster.

4 For each of the following plants, write down which group they are in: a) rose, b) moss and c) pine tree.

5 Write a branching key to identify members of your family. You should include at least four members of your family in the key.

6 Scientists in Outer Mongolia have just discovered an animal which is new to science. On the news, they said it had a mixture of characteristics from a fish and a mammal. There are no photographs of the animal available yet. Draw and label a picture to show what you think the animal looks like.

7 Using the library, the Internet or textbooks, try to find out about other invertebrate phyla. How many invertebrate phyla exist altogether? What are they called? What do they look like? Write a report on your findings.

Feeding relationships

It's strange to think that all of the energy you've used today in moving, thinking, keeping warm and anything else you can think of, came originally from the light of the Sun's rays.

In this chapter, we will find out more about how this energy is transferred and about the feeding relationships between different organisms.

Light energy is absorbed by plants during the process of photosynthesis and stored in chemicals (such as glucose and starch) in their stems and leaves. Biologists refer to plants as **producers** because they make food material which supports animals, bacteria and fungi.

Anything that eats another living thing takes up its energy. Animals that eat plants are known as **herbivores** or **primary consumers**. Animals that eat other animals are known as **carnivores** or **secondary consumers**. A **food chain** is a list of organisms that eat each other. Arrows in the chain show the direction of the flow of energy. A simple food chain that might be found in a garden pond might look like Figure 1.

Figure 1 ▼   A simple food chain for a pond

The top **predator** (like the heron in Figure 1) doesn't get preyed upon, but the energy stored in its body is taken up by **scavengers**, such as maggots, and **decomposers**, such as bacteria and fungi, when it dies.

We can use information about organisms in a particular habitat to make a **pyramid of numbers**.

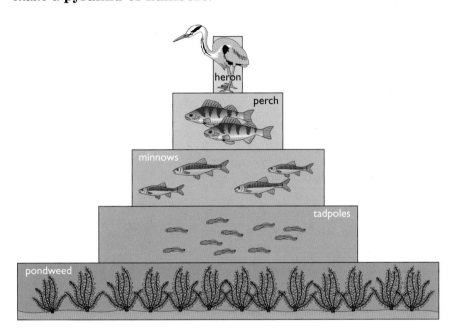

Figure 2 ◀ A pyramid of numbers for the pond food chain

In Figure 2, by far the most numerous organism is the pondweed so it gets the biggest block. The consumers that follow each get a block according to how many there are in that habitat. Pyramids of number normally follow the pattern shown in Figure 2, but sometimes their shape can be quite different. In a woodland habitat, the producers (trees) are so big that they can support high numbers of other organisms that rely upon them for food. This relationship is shown in the food chain below:

Organisms:	Oak trees	Caterpillar	Blackbird	Hawk
Numbers:	10	1000	8	1

In this case the pyramid of numbers looks like the one in Figure 3.

Figure 3 ▼ A pyramid of numbers for a woodland food chain

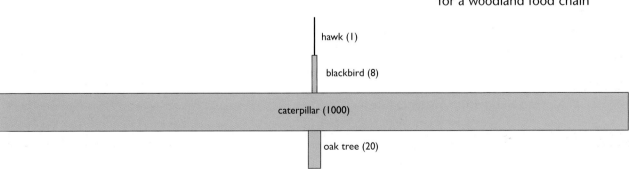

Test Yourself

1 Why are plants known as producers?

2 What do the arrows in food chains represent?

3 Suggest organisms to complete the following food chains:

   a) Grass ⟶ Rabbit ⟶ ?
   b) Lettuce ⟶ Slug ⟶ Blackbird ⟶ ?
   c) Grass ⟶ Deer ⟶ ?
   d) Oak leaves ⟶ Snail ⟶ Hedgehog ⟶ ?

4 Make up pyramids of number to represent the food chains above.

5 What happens to the energy stored in the tissues of the top predators in your food chains?

Food webs

Although food chains are useful, in reality things are usually much more complex as most animals eat more than one type of food. This more complex set of relationships can be shown in a **food web**. The food web in Figure 4 shows some of the complex feeding patterns that occur in the Antarctic Ocean. Like all food webs, it begins with a producer – in this case it's the microscopic plants that live in the ocean called phytoplankton.

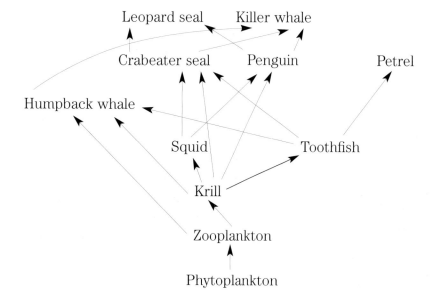

Figure 4 ▲ A food web for the Antarctic Ocean

6   Write out three separate food chains from the food web in Figure 4.

7   Draw a pyramid of numbers for one of these food chains.

8   Name three carnivores and one herbivore from this food web.

9   What do you think would happen to the population of squid if the number of humpback whales suddenly decreased? Explain your answer.

Ideas and Evidence

Pesticides and the food chain

Malaria is a disease that is spread by mosquitoes. It is often fatal. In the 1940s, chemists developed DDT, a pesticide which was very effective at eradicating the mosquito. Safety tests at the time indicated that the small quantities needed to kill insects had no adverse effects on other forms of wildlife. This development was hailed as a breakthrough in public health and DDT was used to kill mosquitoes and other pests throughout the world.

An American marine biologist called Rachel Carson sounded a note of caution in her book *The Silent Spring*. She put forward the idea that a predator that eats lots of prey with a small concentration of pesticide in their tissues, will quickly develop a large concentration of pesticide in its tissues. She called this idea 'biomagnification'.

The chemical companies ridiculed her and accused her of being anti-progress. Rachel stuck to her guns, however, and evidence which supported her idea soon came from studies of Clear Lake in California. Residents living near Clear Lake enjoyed living next to water but were annoyed by the swarms of gnats which bred in the summer months. They decided to use DDD – a pesticide very similar to DDT – to kill the annoying insects. After two applications of the pesticide, people began to notice large numbers of dead grebes (fish-eating birds) on the lake. People were mystified at first as the birds showed no signs of infectious disease. When their tissues were analysed, however, it was found that they contained very high concentrations of pesticide; much higher than was found in the water of the lake.

Figure 5 ▲   Rachel Carson, who first put forward the idea of biomagnification

Pesticides and the food chain continued

It was only when the food chains in the lake were studied that people began to realise that Rachel Carson had been right all along. If you look at the food chain below you'll see that the concentration of DDD in phytoplankton in the lake was indeed tiny – only 0.000003 ppm (ppm means parts per million). The concentration in zooplankton was much higher, because each zooplankton has to eat thousands of phytoplankton to stay alive. Similarly, minnows eat thousands of zooplankton in their lifetime, concentrating the pesticide still further.

This increase in concentration happens again in perch and finally in the grebe whereupon the concentration of pesticide becomes so high that it is enough to kill them.

Similar results were found in many food chains across the United States. The pelican, bald eagle and osprey nearly became extinct as a result of biomagnification. The use of DDT was banned in the USA in 1972 and shortly afterwards in Britain. The population of grebe on the waters of Clear Lake are only now beginning to recover.

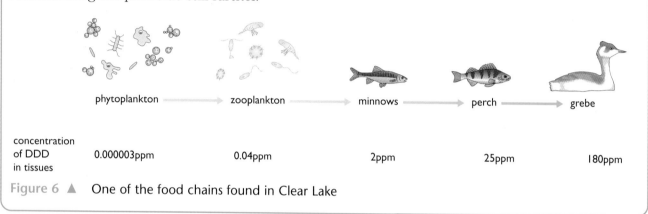

concentration of DDD in tissues	phytoplankton →	zooplankton →	minnows →	perch →	grebe
	0.000003ppm	0.04ppm	2ppm	25ppm	180ppm

Figure 6 ▲ One of the food chains found in Clear Lake

10 Why was DDT first seen as a great benefit to mankind?

11 What does the term 'biomagnification' mean?

12 Explain why the concentration of pesticide in the tissues of the grebe was much higher than that in the tissues of the perch.

13 How many times more concentrated is the pesticide in the tissues of the perch than in the zooplankton?

Predators and prey

A predator is an animal that hunts and kills other animals for food. The animals that it feeds on are known as its **prey**. Figure 7 shows one of the most voracious predators in the ocean. The Great White shark preys on fish, dolphins, porpoises, seals and turtles. You'll be relieved to find out that they rarely attack human beings. Their amazing sense of smell means that they can detect a drop of blood from a distance of a mile!

Figure 7 ▲ The Great White Shark – one of the most successful predators in the world

The mathematics of predators and prey

In the 1920s, an Italian mathematician called Volterra noticed that the number of fishing boats on the Adriatic Sea wasn't constant. When fish were plentiful, more boats arrived, drawn by the success of others. After some time, the number of boats would decrease as fish stocks rapidly diminished due to over-fishing. As the boats went elsewhere, the fish stocks in that region recovered and the cycle repeated itself. This pattern is known as 'boom and bust' and has since been observed in many natural populations.

Ideas and Evidence

The lynx and the snowshoe hare

The snowshoe hare is brilliantly adapted for life in its harsh environment. It has a very thick coat which changes colour from a greyish brown in the summer to white during winter. Its feet are long and wide which allow it to run over snow without sinking. The bottom of its feet are covered with fur which insulates them from the cold and allows them to grip onto the snow. In the summer it eats grass, leaves and buds of trees; in the winter it eats tree bark and twigs.

The lynx is a stealthy and agile member of the cat family. It varies in length between 0.5 and 1.3 metres. It has long, powerful back legs with a bulky body. Like the hare, the lynx's feet are very wide with a layer of hair on the bottom. It preys upon lots of smaller creatures such as mice, squirrels and rats, but is strong and fast enough to catch and kill small deer! Its favourite food by far, however, is the snowshoe hare.

Part of the business of the Hudson Bay Trading Company was to sell the pelts of the lynx and the snowshoe hare. The company kept very careful records of their numbers for more than 100 years. If you look at the graph below, you'll see that there is a definite pattern.

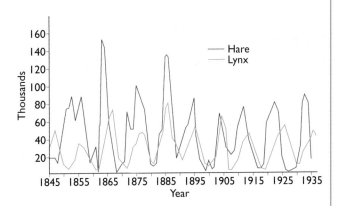

Figure 9 ▲

It's immediately obvious that the number of lynx closely follows the number of hares. It seems that when the number of hares is high, the lynx catch and eat a huge number of them. The lynx population grows rapidly causing a crash in the hare population. When this happens, the lynx run out of food and die of starvation. This in turn allows the hare population to recover and the cycle repeats itself.

Figure 8 ◄　A lynx

14 Name two predators and their prey.

15 Describe how a) the snowshoe hare and b) the lynx are adapted to survive in their environment.

16 Write out a food chain, ending with the lynx, using the information from the above text.

17 Explain why the populations of the lynx and snowshoe hare fluctuate dramatically.

Competition

In the wild, resources such as food, water, light and space are always limited. This leads to **competition** both between members of the same species and between members of different species. Competition can be obvious, such as when lions fight over a recent kill, or it can be subtle, as in the case of a large oak tree shading out the light from other smaller trees. Competition can often lead to the death of weaker or less well adapted members of a species, with the strongest and best adapted gaining access to the best habitats and the most food.

When a new species is introduced to a particular habitat, it will compete with other similar species, often leading to disastrous results for the native species.

The red squirrel vs. the grey squirrel

Figure 10 ▼ The red squirrel has almost disappeared in Britain since the arrival of the grey squirrel

Britain's native squirrel is the red squirrel. Up until the 19th Century, this was the only type of squirrel that lived in our woodlands. In 1876, a pair of American grey squirrels were introduced to Britain at Henbury Park in Cheshire. Soon after this, they were introduced to 30 more sites in the South of England. The grey squirrel did well. By the 1920s it had bred so successfully that it had substantially overtaken our native red squirrel in numbers. It was noticed that whenever grey squirrels moved into the same area as a resident group of red squirrels, the number of red squirrels declined rapidly. This spread of the grey squirrel has continued to such an extent that the red squirrel is now an endangered species in Britain. It is now found mostly only in certain forests in the North of England and Scotland.

It was first thought that the grey squirrels were attacking and killing our native squirrel, or that they carried a disease which killed them. Neither of these suspicions proved to be true. The simple fact is that grey squirrels are far better at competing for natural resources. The factsheets below gives some information about the two species. As you're reading them, try to work out why grey squirrels successfully out-compete our native red squirrel.

The red squirrel

Reproduction: Females have two litters of 2–3 young per year. They can continue producing young up to the age of 6 years.

Eating habits: Food consists of acorns, hazelnuts, pine cones, tree bark and wild cherry.

Notes: Red squirrels are very timid creatures – they are especially shy of humans.

The grey squirrel

Reproduction: Females have two litters per year of 3–4 young. They can continue to produce young up to the age of 9 years.

Eating habits: Food consists of acorns, hazelnuts, pine cones, wild cherry, flowers, insects, frogs, birds' eggs, chicks, remains of human food.

Notes: Compared to the red squirrel, they are confident and not shy of humans, often taking bread out of their hands. It has recently been found that their digestive systems are more efficient at digesting acorns than those of red squirrels.

Test Yourself

20 What resources must plants compete for?

21 List some of the resources that the red and grey squirrel compete for.

22 Why do you think that the introduction of grey squirrels to Britain led to a catastrophic decline in the number of red squirrels?

Summary

When you have finished studying this chapter, you should understand that:

✔ A food chain shows the feeding relationships between organisms in a simple way.

✔ Every food chain starts with a producer which has received its energy from the Sun, for example a green plant.

✔ When the top predator dies, the energy from its body is returned to the environment by scavengers and decomposers.

✔ Pyramids of numbers can be used to show how the numbers of organisms differ at different stages in a food chain.

✔ All food chains have the same structure:

✔ Food webs are a more realistic way of showing the feeding relationships between organisms in a habitat.

✔ Pesticides can build up through food chains by a process called biomagnification and can result in the death of the top predator.

✔ The numbers of predators and prey fluctuate over time in a predictable way.

✔ Organisms compete for resources such as food, water, light and space.

producer ⟶ primary consumer (herbivore) ⟶ secondary consumer (carnivore)

End-of-Chapter Questions

1 Explain in your own words the following key terms you have met in this chapter:

producer

herbivore

primary consumer

carnivore

secondary consumer

food chain

predator

scavenger

decomposer

pyramid of numbers

food web

prey

competition

2 Below are two food chains from separate lakes:

Lake 1:

pondweed ➤ tadpole ➤ minnow ➤ bull trout

Lake 2

pondweed ➤ water beetle ➤ minnow ➤ grey trout ➤ bull trout ➤ pike

a) Draw pyramids of number to represent the food chains in both lakes.

b) A friend of yours has been fishing and has caught a bull trout in each lake. Which lake contains the bull trout most likely to have the highest pesticide concentration? Explain your answer.

c) A new species of trout called the rainbow trout is introduced into both lakes. It is bigger than both the grey trout and bull trout and has the ability to consume a wider variety of prey. Predict what effects the introduction of this new species will have on the ecosystem of each lake.

3 The table below shows the number of Lemmings (a small rodent) and Arctic fox (predator of the lemmings) in an area of tundra in the north of Canada over 10 years.

Year	Lemming numbers	Arctic fox numbers
1991	3500	31
1992	40	12
1993	200	13
1994	4000	40
1995	200	20
1996	150	11
1997	3950	19
1998	3400	38
1999	221	20
2000	14	6
2001	260	8

a) Make a graph to present the data above.

b) Explain why the numbers of lemming and fox vary dramatically from year to year.

c) Why do you think that the fur of the Arctic fox varies from a reddy-brown colour in summer to a white colour in the winter?

4 Your parents are keen gardeners and loathe the slugs that eat their carrots and potatoes. Their solution is to use pesticides called 'slug pellets'. These pellets are very attractive to slugs who eat them and then die. The manufacturers claim that the pellets do not harm birds because they are blue and birds find this colour unappealing and do not eat them as a result.

a) Explain to your parents how they may be unknowingly damaging your garden birds.

b) Investigate alternative strategies to control the slug population. A good place to start your enquiry is at http://www.eartheasy.com/grow_nat_slug_cntrl.htm

Put simply, a **habitat** is a place in which something lives. This place could be the open oceans, a river, a rainforest or, in the case of a tapeworm, your intestines! Different organisms are suited or adapted to the conditions that different habitats present. They have special features which allow them to take advantage of the challenges that face them each day. In this chapter, we will see some of the **adaptations** that particular organisms have which help them to survive in their habitat.

The intertidal zone

The gravitational pull of the moon upon the sea causes gigantic waves which sometimes break as they travel along rivers. Figure 1 shows surfers riding the tidal wave of the river Severn.

Figure 1 ◀ Surfers on the Severn bore

This daily change in sea levels, with tides changing approximately every 6 hours, creates a habitat that presents lots of challenges to anything that lives there. The very edge of the sea, the part that becomes covered and uncovered by water as the tide ebbs and flows, is known as the **intertidal zone**.

The organisms that live here have to be able to cope with extreme daily changes. One of the most successful of these is the barnacle. If you've ever walked barefoot over a rocky shoreline, you'll know what I'm talking about. These are the creatures that seem to be part of the rock itself, covering nearly every bit of it. You barely think about this animal as you gingerly pick your way over them, but their life cycle is extremely strange...

When they first emerge from their eggs, barnacles look like tiny shrimps. They swim around like this for about a month, eating the tiny plant plankton which floats in the sea. They then undergo a weird transformation, changing into an egg-shaped organism that doesn't actually feed at all.

The barnacle exists in this state for about 13 days before looking for a place to attach itself. The young barnacle then makes a sticky substance on one of its appendages and it uses this to glue itself to the rock – in fact it glues itself down upon its head! Within 12 hours another strange change takes place. The barnacle builds a shell around itself made up of six plates. The adult spends the rest of its life glued upside down to the rock. This glue is strong enough so that even the biggest waves that batter the coastline cannot dislodge the barnacle.

When the tide goes out, the barnacle closes the four top plates of its shell, ensuring that it will not dry out. When the tide comes in, these plates are opened and the barnacle uses its legs to grab passing bits of food and sweep them down into its mouth. Its legs have got special sensory hairs which can feel for the plankton, and gills to absorb oxygen from the water.

Figure 2 ▲   The intertidal zone – home of the barnacle

The barnacle grows most during the spring and summer, when the increased hours of daylight mean that there is plenty of plant plankton to be eaten. It does this by adding new bits to the outside of the shell and digesting the inside of the shell to allow room for expansion.

The barnacle reproduces during the spring and summer – which is tricky when you're stuck to a rock by your head. It achieves this by a remarkable set of adaptations:

- the barnacle is a **hermaphrodite** which means that it has male and female reproductive organs.
- in relation to its body size, the barnacle's penis is the longest of any living thing on the planet. If you scaled it up to human size it would be nine metres in length!

When it's time to reproduce, the barnacle uncoils its penis, pokes it out of its shell and searches for the perfect partner. It then pushes the penis into the other barnacle's shell and deposits its sperm. The eggs are fertilised and then released into the ocean.

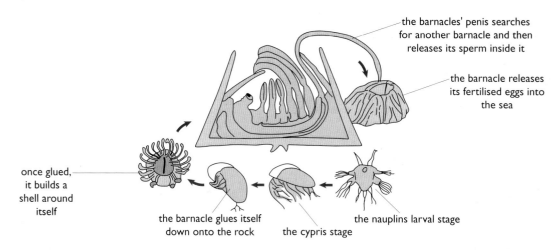

the barnacles' penis searches for another barnacle and then releases its sperm inside it

the barnacle releases its fertilised eggs into the sea

once glued, it builds a shell around itself

the barnacle glues itself down onto the rock

the cypris stage

the nauplins larval stage

Figure 3 ▲ The stages in the life cycle of a barnacle

Test Yourself

1 Name as many different kinds of habitat as you can, listing some of the animals and plants that live there.

2 What causes tides?

3 a) Describe the barnacle's habitat.
b) What challenges does the habitat present to anything that lives there?

4 Copy and complete the following table. The first line has been completed for you.

Adaptation	Survival value
the barnacle makes a strong glue	to ensure it doesn't become dislodged by waves
a plated shell that it can open and close	
sensory hairs on its legs	
gills on its legs	
they reproduce only in spring and summer	
very long penis	

Deciduous Forests

Britain has a temperate climate. This means that it's not very warm or very cold and we have four distinct seasons – spring, summer, autumn and winter.

Figure 4 ◄ A deciduous wood in Britain

Figure 5 ▲ Each of these rings represents one year of the tree's growth

Most of the trees that grow in Britain are called 'deciduous', which means they lose their leaves in the autumn and regrow them in the spring.

During the autumn, the amount of daylight that we get starts to diminish and the trees respond by extracting the chlorophyll (the pigment responsible for photosynthesis) from the leaves. Once the chlorophyll has been extracted, you can see the other pigments that exist in the leaves, producing beautiful orange, yellow and reddish shades. Once the leaves have changed colour, they drop off the tree. Deciduous trees do this to save resources, as there isn't enough light to photosynthesise effectively in the winter months. Trees only grow in the spring and summer months, which results in growth rings. Each ring represents one year of growth so you can work out the age of a tree simply by counting the rings in its trunk.

The oak tree relies upon the wind to disperse its pollen and has large catkins with lots of anthers making millions of pollen grains. Researchers have found that oak pollen is dispersed better on dry days. Oaks don't release their pollen until the humidity is less than 45%. The fruit that the oak tree produces are called acorns. The production of acorns is timed to coincide with squirrels' need to store a cache of them to see them through the winter. Naturally, the squirrels forget where they hid some acorns and these grow into oak trees. Nobody knows exactly how oak trees do this, but it is thought that they 'know' the time of year by detecting changes in the length of the day and air temperature.

Apart from the challenge of dealing with the changing seasons, a tree has to adapt to the daily movement of the Sun across the sky. Trees have the ability to angle their leaves in order to maximise the amount of light hitting them. You may also have noticed that trees bend away from shaded areas towards the light as they grow.

Some plants, such as bluebells and daffodils, grow in early spring to ensure that they don't have to compete with the larger trees for light.

Test Yourself

5   Describe what the countryside looks like in spring, summer, autumn and winter.

6   Why do deciduous trees lose their leaves in autumn?

7   What causes the colour changes in autumn leaves?

8   What adaptations do trees have to maximise the amount of photosynthesis that occurs?

9   Why don't you see bluebells in late summer?

10 What signals are detected by oak trees to indicate the time of year?

11 How do you think oak trees distinguish between spring and autumn?

Figure 6 ▲ Woodland flowers, like bluebells and daffodils, flower in early spring before the trees have grown leaves

Humans' effect on the Earth

Human beings are unusual – we are not specifically adapted for any particular habitat. Instead, we make tools and houses for ourselves to modify our own environment. We are so successful at this that our species is found on every continent on the planet. We are able to survive under the oceans, in the skies and even in space. This ability to change our surroundings to suit ourselves has meant that the human population has been able to grow dramatically, especially during the 20th Century.

Figure 7 ▼ As far as we know, the Earth is the only planet in our Solar System capable of supporting life

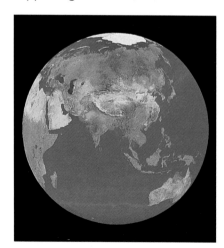

During the last century, advances in farming, public health and medicine meant that more people survived into old age and less people died in childbirth than was previously the case. The current estimate is that five new human beings are born every second of the day. In the same time, two people die. This means that the population of the Earth is increasing by three every second. You can see the current population estimate at: www.census.gov/ipc/www/world.html.

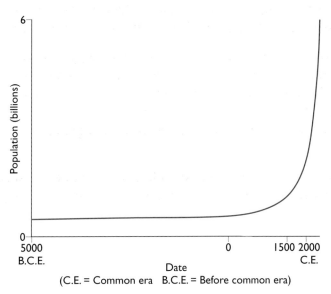

Date
(C.E. = Common era   B.C.E. = Before common era)

Figure 8 ▲   This graph shows how the human population has grown in the last 1200 years

Wherever humans live, however, they have an impact upon their surroundings. We dig up rocks and cut down trees to build houses, roads and walls. We burn trees and fossil fuels to heat our houses. We clear large areas of forest to make pasture on which to graze our animals and we create vast quantities of waste which we tend to dump in landfill sites. All of these activities reduce the space available for other living things.

Sometimes, humans bring new organisms with them as they colonise new areas. This often has dramatic effects upon the native animals and plants that live there...

Ideas and Evidence   The sad tale of the dodo

Mauritius is an island off the East coast of Africa which remained completely uninhabited by human beings until the 16th Century. Portuguese sailors were the first people to attempt to settle on the island, followed by the Dutch and finally the French. They encountered strange plants and animals not found anywhere else on the planet. One of these was a large, plump, flightless bird called the dodo.

Figure 9 ▶   A dodo

Ideas and Evidence

The sad tale of the dodo continued

Dodos had never seen human beings before. In fact they had no natural predators on the island. Because of this, they were not adapted to run away from the sailors that came ashore. Unfortunately for the dodo, the sailors saw them as a ready source of food and killed thousands of them.

Rats, previously absent from the island, came ashore from the ship and ate the dodos' eggs. This was easy for them as dodos made their nests on the ground. The combined effect of the sailors and the rats meant that the dodos became extinct within 100 years. Of the 45 species of birds originally found on Mauritius, only 19 of them survived the colonisation.

An unexpected effect of the extinction of the dodo was that a certain type of tree, the *Calvaria major* tree, also started diminishing in numbers. It was noticed fairly recently that all of the trees left of this type (numbering no more than 13) were more than 300 years old. Apparently, the dodo ate the fruit of this tree, and its digestive system removed the seed's thick coating. Only after going through the dodo's digestive system would the seed germinate. Luckily, some scientists noticed that turkeys' digestive systems have a similar effect and the tree seems to have been saved from extinction.

The arrival of human beings led to a decrease in the **biodiversity** of the island. 'Biodiversity' means the number of different species of animals and plants that live in a particular habitat.

Test Yourself

12 Why are human beings able to live on every continent on the planet?

13 How do humans reduce the amount of space available for other living things?

14 Explain why the human population started to increase rapidly during the 20th Century.

15 Why did the dodo become extinct?

16 Why did the Calvaria tree begin to decline in numbers after the dodo's extinction?

17 What does the term biodiversity mean?

The Amazonian rainforests

The Amazonian rainforest has the highest level of biodiversity on Earth. Nearly half of the world's species of plants, animals and micro-organisms live here, yet it is being destroyed at a rate of one and a half acres (one and a half football pitches) per second.

Land in the rainforest can be bought very cheaply, so ranchers clear vast areas, selling the wood to make furniture, to construct houses and to make paper for newspapers and magazines. They can then grow crops on that area, but because the soil of rainforests is so poor in nutrients, farmers cannot reuse the land year upon year. They have to cut more of the forest down to carry on growing their crops, destroying the forest piece by piece.

Figure 10 ▲ The effect of logging on the Amazonian rainforest has been devastating

Mass extinction

Biologists estimate that 137 species of plants, animals and insects are becoming **extinct** every day because of the destruction of the rainforest. In itself this makes distressing reading, but there are practical as well as emotional reasons to be concerned about this loss.

Figure 11 ▼ The greenhouse effect

Around 50% of the medicines that are prescribed in the western world are derived from plants. For example the heart drug 'digitalis' comes from the foxglove and 'aspirin' comes from willow trees. More than half of these drugs are derived from rainforest plants, yet only 1% of rainforest plants have been tested by pharmaceutical companies. The mass extinction we are currently witnessing may be leading to the loss of important drugs which could cure life-threatening diseases.

Rainforests absorb a huge amout of carbon dioxide from the air during the process of photosynthesis. It's important that they continue to do this because carbon dioxide has

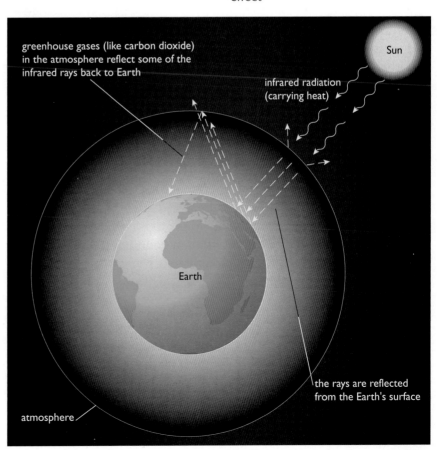

greenhouse gases (like carbon dioxide) in the atmosphere reflect some of the infrared rays back to Earth

Sun

infrared radiation (carrying heat)

Earth

the rays are reflected from the Earth's surface

atmosphere

the effect of warming the planet in the phenomenon known as the **greenhouse effect**. Carbon dioxide reflects infrared radiation (which carries heat energy) back to Earth. The more carbon dioxide there is in our atmosphere, the hotter the Earth becomes. Destruction of the rainforest means that less carbon dioxide can be absorbed and the planet could become hotter as a result, leading to the melting of the polar ice caps and subsequent increase in sea levels.

Test Yourself

18 List all the products you can think of that are made out of wood.

19 Why do farmers in the Amazon clear so much forest?

20 Calculate how many acres of rainforest have been destroyed in the last 5 minutes.

21 Why is the preservation of rainforests important to human beings?

Sustainability

During the early 1960s, the science of ecology was born. Environmentalists began to argue that the health of all living things on the planet was connected. Most industries that developed during the 20th Century ignored their effects on the local environment, with many habitats being destroyed and thousands of species becoming extinct as a result. In the 21st Century, businesses are now being encouraged to think about how to be profitable without damaging the environment. This is known as **sustainable development**.

To be sustainable a business should be economically efficient, protect and restore habitats, and enhance the well-being of everyone. A sustainable business recognises the importance of leaving the world in a good condition for the benefit of future generations – that's you and any children that you might have!

There are sustainable alternatives to cutting down the rainforest to satisfy our demand for wood. A company in Nova Scotia has decided to harvest trees from existing forests using an old fashioned method called 'single tree selection'. This method identifies individual trees within a forest for harvesting. The trees selected will be unhealthy, fully grown, of poor quality or ones which are shading others and therefore slowing their growth.

Figure 12 ▲ Single tree selection – a sustainable way of harvesting wood

Figure 13 ▲ This method is known as clear cutting. It destroys large areas of forest very quickly

Using horses means that no new roads need to be built to allow access for heavy vehicles, so damage to the forest will be minimal.

Contrast this method with modern industrial forestry whereby large areas of forest are indiscriminantly mown down by huge machinery, leaving vast empty areas without any trees. Not only does this method disrupt the habitat for many plants and animals, it also damages the quality of the soil. Heavy machinery churns the soil up so that when the rain comes, the nutrients get washed away leaving a poorer quality soil for future planting of trees.

Test Yourself

22 What does the term 'sustainable development' mean?

23 Why is 'single tree selection' a more sustainable form of forestry than 'clear cutting'?

24 Make a table in your books showing which of the following practises will preserve biodiversity and which will decrease biodiversity:

making nest boxes for birds, leaving litter on the floor, cutting hedgerows in autumn rather than spring (think about berries!), recycling paper, quarrying, mining, using wind farms to make electricity, dredging sand from the sea bed.

Summary

When you have finished studying this chapter, you should understand that:

✓ A habitat is a place where an organism lives.

✓ Organisms have developed adaptations to help them survive in their particular habitat.

✓ Human beings are unusual in that they can survive in any habitat and can be found on every continent on the planet.

✓ The human population is increasing by three people every second of the day.

✓ The increase in the human population has had a devastating effect on the planet.

✓ Around 137 species of plants, animals and insects are becoming extinct every day as a result of the destruction of the Amazonian rainforest.

✓ The removal of such vast quantities of trees has contributed to the greenhouse effect.

✓ Humans must now concentrate on sustainable development – which means making a profit without damaging the environment.

End-of-Chapter Questions

1 Explain in your own words the following key terms you have met in this chapter:

habitat

adaptation

intertidal zone

hermaphrodite

biodiversity

extinct

greenhouse effect

sustainable development

2 The Dromedary camel is a mammal that is adapted to live in the deserts of Northern Africa. During the day, temperatures can rise to 45°C and rainfall is extremely scarce. The camel has several adaptations to enable it to live in these conditions, some of which are listed in the table below. Copy the table and suggest some possible benefits for each one.

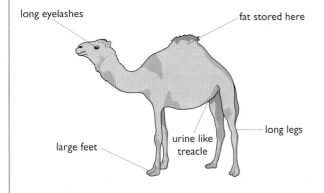

long eyelashes

fat stored here

long legs

urine like treacle

large feet

Adaptation	Benefits
fat stored in hump (rather than around whole of body)	
very long legs	
camel produces urine so concentrated that it flows like treacle	
large, two-toed foot	
very long eyelashes	

3 Cacti are the most successful plants which live in the desert. Listed in the table below are some of their adaptations. Suggest the survival value of each one.

Adaptation	Survival value
leaves shrunken to tiny spines	
a large network of roots spreading out near the surface of the soil	
a thick waxy coating	

4 A crisp manufacturer has decided to make its bags from cellulose (made from plant cell walls) instead of plastic. Bacteria in the soil can break down cellulose into simpler materials such as carbon dioxide, water and nutrients that plants can absorb. Design an advertisment selling the environmental benefits of such a change to the general public.

5 Your parents have decided to buy a dining room table made from mahogany. This is a tree which only grows in tropical rainforests and takes hundreds of years to reach maturity. How could you persuade them to buy a sustainable alternative?

6 Imagine that you are a research scientist for a large pharmaceutical company. Your research has led you to believe that a rare plant that grows only in the Amazonian Rainforest produces a chemical which could possibly cure skin cancer. How would you set about investigating this possibility?

Index

Note: Page numbers in *italics* refer to illustrations.

Photo Acknowledgements

The publishers would like to thank the following individuals, institutions and companies for permission to reproduce photographs in this book. Every effort has been made to trace ownership of copyright. The publishers would be happy to make arrangements with any copyright holder whom it has not been possible to contact:

Action Plus (25 top, 36, 58 top); Anna Maloney (114 bottom right); Biophoto Associates (22); Bruce Coleman (1 top right, 2, 43, 114 bottom left, 123 all, 131, 132 bottom 3, 144, 145, 146 both); Corbis (68, 74, 114 top right, 143, 155); GSF Picture Library (93); Hodder and Stoughton (1 top two left, bottom left, 114 all 4 in top left); Holt (5 middle, 21 both, 75 top, 92 both, 95 both, 97, 99 both, 107 both, 110, 153 right); Life File (1 bottom right, 25 bottom, 26 both, 39, 100, 153 left, 154 top); Network Photographers/Homer Sykes (103); Redfern (127 all); Royal Geographical Society (65 both); Science Museum/Science and Society Picture Library (7); Science Photo Library (1 middle left, middle right, 5 top, bottom left and right, 6, 7 top and bottom, 15 all, 18, 19, 27, 32, 38 both, 42, 45, 46, 49 all, 50 all, 58 bottom, 69, 73 bottom, 75 bottom, 80 both, 83, 86, 88, 89, 119 both, 120, 122, 132 top, 151, 154 bottom); Still Pictures (76, 77, 157, 158 both); Wellcome Trust (73 top); West Media (150).

Index by Indexing Specialists

Orders: please contact Bookpoint Ltd, 130 Milton Park, Abingdon, Oxon OX14 4SB. Telephone: (44) 01235 827720, Fax: (44) 01235 400454. Lines are open from 9.00 – 6.00, Monday to Saturday, with a 24 hour message answering service. Email address: orders@bookpoint.co.uk

British Library Cataloguing in Publication Data
A catalogue record for this title is available from The British Library

ISBN 0 340 80476 9

First published 2002
Impression number 10 9 8 7 6 5 4 3 2 1
Year   2008 2007 2006 2005 2004 2003 2002

Cover photo from Science Photo Library.
Typeset by Fakenham Photosetting Ltd.
Printed in Italy for Hodder & Stoughton Educational, a division of Hodder Headline Plc, 338 Euston Road, London NW1 3BH.